Pay It Down!

PAY IT DOWN!

From Debt to Wealth
on $10 a Day

Jean Chatzky

PORTFOLIO

PORTFOLIO

Published by the Penguin Group

Penguin Group (USA) Inc., 375 Hudson Street, New York, New York 10014, U.S.A.

Penguin Group (Canada), 10 Alcorn Avenue, Toronto, Ontario, Canada M4V 3B2
(a division of Pearson Penguin Canada Inc.)

Penguin Books Ltd, 80 Strand, London WC2R 0RL, England

Penguin Ireland, 25 St Stephen's Green, Dublin 2, Ireland (a division of Penguin
Books Ltd)

Penguin Books Australia Ltd, 250 Camberwell Road, Camberwell, Victoria 3124,
Australia (a division of Pearson Australia Group Pty Ltd)

Penguin Books India Pvt Ltd, 11 Community Centre, Panchsheel Park, New
Delhi–110 017, India

Penguin Group (NZ), Cnr Airborne and Rosedale Roads, Albany, Auckland,
New Zealand (a division of Pearson New Zealand Ltd)

Penguin Books (South Africa) (Pty) Ltd, 24 Sturdee Avenue, Rosebank, Johan-
nesburg 2196, South Africa

Penguin Books Ltd, Registered Offices: 80 Strand, London WC2R 0RL, England

First published in 2004 by Portfolio, a member of Penguin Group (USA) Inc.

10   9   8   7   6

PUBLISHER'S NOTE

This publication is designed to provide accurate and authoritative information
in regard to the subject matter covered. It is sold with the understanding that
the publisher is not engaged in rendering legal, accounting or other professional services. If you require legal advice or other expert assistance, you
should seek the services of a competent professional.

LIBRARY OF CONGRESS CATALOGING–IN–PUBLICATION DATA

Chatzky, Jean Sherman———
    Pay it down! : from debt to wealth on $10 a day / Jean Chatzky.
        p. cm.
    Includes index.
    ISBN 1-59184-063-5
    1. Consumer credit. 2. Finance, Personal. 3. Debt. I. Title.

HG3755.C484 2004
332.024'02—dc22   2004040109

This book is printed on acid-free paper. ∞

Printed in the United States of America

Designed by Carla Bolte • Set in Nofret

For Patricia—and everyone else who deserves a new beginning.

THE PROMISE

H ow would you like to be free of overwhelming credit card debt? To have a financial cushion to fall back on? To know you have the skills to save and invest for any goal—and to guarantee your financial future?

I can teach you how to get there on $10 a day. If that sounds like very little, well it is.

It's a movie—without popcorn.

It's lunch at McDonald's—for two children.

It's skipping the car wash—and washing the car in your driveway instead.

It's so many of those things that you can do without. But it's also the key to your future. Let's say you're the average American. You have a decent job, but you also have $8,000 in high-rate credit card debt. You have no savings to speak of. You worry about your money on a daily basis (in fact, it keeps you up at night), and you don't believe that $10 a day can dig you out of that hole. But it can, and in less time than you may think. If you get on this plan—and stick with it:

In 3 years...you'll be credit–card–free. By applying that $10 a day against your $8,000 credit card debt (at an interest rate of 16 percent), you'll be debt–free in 33 months.

In 5 years...you'll have a financial cushion. Once the debt is gone, you can start saving that $10 a day for your future. You'll put the money in a money-market account. It won't earn much in interest while it's sitting there, but there's no risk you'll lose it either. Five years from the time you started socking away your $10 a day, you'll have a fat emergency cushion—more than $8,000. That's your insurance against a leaky roof, a layoff or illness, or other financial mishap that comes your way.

In 10 years...you'll have a nest egg for retirement. After your emergency cushion is in place, you can start investing your $10 a day so that it can work harder and grow faster for your benefit. If you put it somewhere that it can grow tax-free—like a 401(k) account—and you earn, on that money, the 10.7 percent that the S&P 500 has returned between 1926 and today, in 10 years...you have $23,994; in 15 years from the day you started, you have $64,866; in 20 years, you have $134,487; in 25 years, you have $253,080; in 30 years, you have $455,091; in 35 years, you have $799,197; and in 40 years, you have $1,385,351.

Nearly $1.4 million on $10 a day. That's real money in anybody's book.

It sounds simple, and it is. All that's standing in your way is knowledge. You need to know how to free up that $10 a day. You need to know how to get your-self to do that every day, without fail, for the rest of your life. And you need to know how to guarantee that that money gets to where it's supposed to be so that it can work its magic for you.

The answers are in the next 200 pages. Read on.

Contents

Introduction:

Getting Ahead and Staying Ahead

52 million times a day.
2.2 million times an hour.
36,242 times a minute.
604 times a second.

That's how often we use our credit cards in this country. That's how often we whip out our slim pieces of plastic, slide them through the little electronic slots or hand them over to the cashier. We type the numbers into our browsers or read them hurriedly to a clerk over the telephone to buy books, or groceries, or movie tickets, or even to foot the bill for the co-payment at the pediatrician's office. We do it so often, we don't even think about it anymore.

But we should. Because on average, each of those transactions costs us $82. That may not sound like much—dinner for four at the local Italian joint; a sweater and a pair of jeans at the Gap; a rehab for the broken vacuum cleaner—but when we start to add up all of those $82 charges, the number quickly becomes meaningful. And when we lump them with the money we owe on our mortgages, our car loans, our home equity loans, and our student loans, the numbers start to get very large very quickly. In fact, they get downright scary.

The fact is, consumer debt, as measured by the Federal Reserve, is at an all-time high. Members of the average household in America owe more than $8,000 on the 16 (16!) pieces of plastic they carry in their wallets. We have less equity in our homes than at any time in the past. We have less equity in our cars than at any time in the past. That's why it's not so surprising that the number of cars repossessed and homes foreclosed on has skyrocketed in recent years. Ditto the number of people filing for bankruptcy.

The fact is, Americans are addicted to debt.

Is Debt Getting in the Way of Your Future?

If you have too much debt—particularly credit card debt—I can guarantee that you don't have much of a financial future. Why? Think about what happens when you have credit card bills looming large. You feel like you *have* to pay those bills first—and so you do. If you don't, the creditors start to call.

Because those bills are so large (even the minimums look maximum), there's nothing left over to save or invest. So when an emergency hits—whether it's an unreimbursed medical bill or a new transmission—you pay for it with plastic. Then the minimums go even higher, and the cycle continues.

There are millions and millions of Americans in your shoes, and, unfortunately, for many, many people it's about to get worse. Years of the lowest interest rates in history have made it possible for you to borrow more for less: you could take out bigger mortgages, larger car loans, tack on home equity lines and keep your monthly payments fairly steady. But interest rates aren't headed down. They aren't even likely to remain fixed for very long. As our improving economy gains traction, they'll be heading up, which means that your adjustable-rate loans—your adjustable-rate mortgage, your home equity line of credit, your variable-rate credit cards—are going to be more expensive.

That's going to be extremely difficult to deal with . . . unless you start to wipe out the most expensive of those debts: your credit card bills.

Why You Have to Tackle the Credit Card Bills First

The amount you can accumulate by investing that $10 a day is so tempting that you'll want to skip the first two steps—the credit card repayment, the emergency savings cushion—and jump right in. (And if you can free up $20 a day, well, then, be my guest.) But there's a good reason for tackling those credit card bills first: at 14, 15, or 16 percent and higher, they're costing you more than you can earn by socking the money away. At 24, 25, or 29 percent, they're costing you double or triple what you can earn. Not only that: they're doing damage to your confidence. They're sabotaging your ability to be content, not only with your money, but with your life. They have to go.

I can make you this promise: As soon as you start plowing through those credit card bills, as soon as you see the numbers heading down rather than up, you're going to feel better. You're not only going to feel optimistic about your financial future, you're going to actually feel, for the first time in a very long time, as if you really have one.

Pay It Down!

STEP 1

Assess the Problem

How Did You Get into This Mess?

Before you can solve any problem, you need to understand how you got into trouble in the first place. That's the only way you can clear up your mess—in this case, your debt mess—and dramatically reduce your chances of it happening again.

So, I want you to think back. At some point, you had a clean credit record. For some of you, that may have been way back when a solicitor approached you on your college campus and offered you a big bag of M&Ms or a T-shirt if you'd apply for a credit card. But for most people, it was sometime later than that. Think what was it that sparked the trouble:

Maybe it was when you lost a job. You may be one of the

2.4 million Americans who've lost a job since 1991. Unfortunately, it now takes longer than ever before to find a new one, and even when you do find a new one, it may come at a lower salary, with no health insurance.

Or when you didn't get the raise you were counting on. Perhaps you made a habit of spending ahead of your salary. You figured that although you earned $35,000 a year this year, you'd earn $40,000 the next year and $45,000 the year after that, so you could afford a more expensive mortgage payment or car payment or wardrobe. But the raises never came—not just for you, but for many people. Over the last few years, the average income for moderate-income families has grown almost imperceptibly.

Maybe it was when you bought your house. The house. Of course you always wanted one. It's always been the American dream. In the past half-decade or so, as the stock market has dawdled, the perception has also been that it's a sure-thing investment. Unfortunately, that's just not the case. Today, so many people are buying houses that they can't truly afford that the foreclosure rate is higher than it's ever been.

Or when you rented your apartment. Between 1993 and 2000, rents rose at twice the rate of inflation. They rose well ahead of the raise you were likely to receive on the job. As your rent ate up a bigger share of your budget each month, maybe you started leaning on your credit cards.

Or when you got divorced. After a divorce, the temptation to try to maintain your standard of living—often by continuing to live in the house you shared with a spouse—is great. Unfortunately, unless you're wealthy, it's also next to impossible.

Maybe it was when you had a health scare. Forty million Americans have no health insurance. Perhaps you're in that boat, but even if you're not, the rising cost of health care can easily throw you deep into debt. Health care premiums have skyrocketed in the last decade. Simultaneously, the percentage of people who had employers paying for that health care fell out of the sky.

Maybe you could afford most of these things, but nothing else. Americans have started using their credit cards to fill the gap between how much they earn and how much they need to live. They may be able to pay their rent, their utilities and their car payments, but groceries, doctors' visits and other necessities are going on the credit card.

Maybe you had no savings to bail you out of a jam. Perhaps the transmission died, or the roof sprung a leak, or you had some other problem that absolutely, positively had to be taken care of but you had no savings to pay for it. So you had to charge it and figure you'd pay it back later, but the cost of living got in the way.

Maybe you have a spending problem. There are people who are addicted to shopping, and then there are people who just spend more than they make. More and more people every year fall into the latter category. According to a Roper survey, fewer Americans in 2004 than in the two previous years said they planned to cut back when it comes to buying luxuries, high-tech items, eating out in restaurants or buying items for their homes. Unfortunately, if you're spending more than you make, you're digging deeper and deeper into debt.

Maybe It Was a Combination of Things

In January 2004, I announced on the *Today* show that later in the year, I would be doing a series on getting out of debt. We would follow—and help—two families in their quest to become debt-free. Then I asked for volunteers. I got thousands of e-mails within

24 hours (if I didn't know I was on the right track already, I knew it then).

What these e-mails showed, time after time after time, was that you are often able to handle a single one of these problems, but, as Murphy's Law would have it, the problems often hit you simultaneously—or one right after the other. You could handle the fact that you had a spending problem as long as you had a high five-figure salary. But then you lost your job. You could handle the fact that you could just barely afford your mortgage payments, until you had a health scare that saddled you with a pile of bills. You thought you could handle the second lease on the second car, until you didn't get that raise you were counting on.

Elizabeth in Washington wrote: "My financial despair is due in part to a devastating personal loss, which resulted in loss of employment. The loss of my job and the resultant stress of the financial devastation it created further impacted my personal loss. I have been suffering from depression and doing some self-medicating with occasional 'retail therapy.' This behavior worsens my situation and leaves me feeling further overwhelmed by my financial situation. I don't know how to 'get a grip'!"

And from Gloria in Pennsylvania: "Two years ago, my husband was forced to retire after 33 years of employment at a local company. When the 'retirement' occurred, we were in the midst of building an addition [to our home], starting a new business and paying for my daughter's wedding. We accumulated $17,000 in credit card debt. Our income, since the retirement, is reduced by almost two-thirds. Both my husband and I work long hours in a seemingly fruitless attempt to pay down our debt; however, the credit card balances remain almost stationary because of the high interest rates, finance fees and late fees. We are drowning."

The sort of worry and anxiety that Elizabeth and Gloria expressed ran through just about every one of the e-mails I received. It also showed up in the results of a RoperASW study conducted at the end of 2003:

- More than 70 percent of people are worried about the rising cost of health care.
- More than 60 percent are worried about having enough money to live "right."
- More than 60 percent are worried about having enough money to pay the bills.
- More than 50 percent are worried about interest rates rising.

Worrying, unfortunately, doesn't do any good, nor does an underlying belief that credit cards are bad or evil. Research by Sue Eccles, a professor at Lancaster University Management School in Great Britain, has shown that most of us believe we use credit too often. Another study by Thomas Durkin, an economist with the Federal Reserve of New York, showed that the more people use their credit cards, the more they feel credit is "bad."

Credit, it turns out, is like a double bacon-cheeseburger (with the bun): we know perfectly well that it's bad for us, and yet we eat it anyway.

So, How Bad Is It?

It's time to answer the question, How much debt *do* you have? Many people really don't know, and even if they do, sometimes their spouses don't. (I got e-mails from people who *wanted* to be "outed" on the *Today* show because they couldn't tell their spouses that they were hiding a massive credit card bill.)

To get on the road to repayment, you need to know how much debt you're carrying and at what interest rates. And if you're part of a couple, you both need to know.

You can use the work sheet on pages 9–10 to get you going or you can do the work on a computer or on another piece of paper, but it's time to take stock.

There are two basic types of debts. *Secured debt* is debt that has an asset—also called collateral—backing it up. Your mortgage is a secured debt that uses your house as collateral. If you miss enough mortgage payments, the bank will foreclose and take your house. Your car loan is, similarly, a secured debt. If you stop writing checks to GM Capital (or whomever), you can count on a visit from the repo man. Likewise, if you've purchased furniture or appliances on a payment plan, this is a secured loan. *Unsecured debts*, on the other hand, are those not backed with collateral. Because there are no assets behind these loans, the bank or lender takes a bigger risk in lending you the money. Nothing can be easily taken from you to force you to pay. That's why the interest rates on unsecured loans are higher. Credit card debts are, as you probably figured, unsecured loans.

When you've completed the work sheet your tendency is going to be to worry. Don't. I know your total looks big. I'm going to teach you how to break it down into manageable pieces so that you can tackle it on $10 a day.

SECURED DEBTS

	Lender	Amount Owed	Term	Rate	Fixed or Variable?
Mortgage					
Home equity loan					
Home equity line of credit					
Car loan					
Boat loan					
Furniture/appliance payment					
Time share					
Other					

Amount owed subtotal: $ _____

9

UNSECURED DEBTS

	Lender	Amount Owed	Term	Rate	Fixed or Variable?
Credit Card 1					
Credit Card 2					
Credit Card 3					
Credit Card 4					
Credit Card 5					
Credit Card 6					
Personal loan					
Other					

Amount owed subtotal: $ _____

TOTAL OWED: $ _____

Tales of Life and Debt:
"We Didn't Know How Bad It Was"

Until very recently, Tina and Brian, parents of two living in Everett, Washington, could tell you that they
were in debt (the bills each month were nonstop and
overwhelming) and they could tell you *why* they were
in debt (Brian lost his job as a help-desk analyst nine
months earlier, cutting their family income in half).
What they couldn't tell you—because they didn't
know themselves—was how bad the problem was.

"If I say I didn't want to know, does that make
sense?" Tina asked. "I'm kind of scared to figure out
where we are. Not knowing somehow makes you feel
better." Unfortunately, not knowing how much you
owe, to whom and at what interest rate allows you to
spend as if the problem doesn't exist, as Tina and Brian
did the previous holiday season. It leaves you won-
dering if you're making the right decisions about who
to pay first. In other words, it gives you room to hang
yourself.

There are many, many people in Brian and Tina's
situation. According to research conducted in late 2002
by RoperASW, although 88 percent of Americans
have enough money to make their rent or mortgage

payments every month and nearly as many have enough money to buy the things they need, only 44 percent can afford to pay off their credit cards each month, and only 32 percent say they'd have enough saved to weather a financial hardship. If you're one of the people who are leaning a little too hard on the plastic in their wallets, step one in getting out of debt is understanding why you're in debt and how bad the problem is.

It comes down to basic psychology: if you don't fix the underlying problem, conquering the symptoms will do you no good in the long run. You'll repeat the destructive behavior and end up in the same debt hole all over again. You need to understand why it happened in the first place. The second thing you need to understand is how bad the problem is. With my prodding, Tina spent a weekend figuring out how much was coming in each month, how much was going out, and where it was going. "It took hours," she said. "I cried."

Tina figured that, with Brian's unemployment checks, they had a net income each month of $4,634. Their average spending for the previous couple of months—which included making the minimum payments on five credit cards, as well as paying the mortgage, a consolidation loan, and home equity line of credit—had been $5,875. "It's even worse than I thought it was," Tina said.

But going through the numbers also showed her the possibilities. Her credit cards were at fairly high interest rates; she vowed to try to reduce those. She also had been spending more than she probably had to for auto and homeowners' insurance, as well as for long-distance phone service. She decided she could easily swap from premium cable to cheaper basic, and she'd never thought of contacting the pricey preschool her daughter attended to ask for financial aid.

The family's goal for the next few months was to trim their expenses to the point where they could at least tread water. Brian enrolled in a training program for medical transcriptionists. He'll graduate and—they believe—will be back in the workforce within six months. By paring their spending back, they can put themselves in position to make rapid progress on their debt when Brian begins working again. And while daunting, that's a prospect that feels good. "I should have done this years ago," Tina said.

STEP 2

Break Your Challenge into Manageable Steps

L ET'S SAY that instead of trying to get out of debt you were trying to lose a little weight before your high school reunion, two months from now. How would you approach that problem? You'd probably climb on the scale and see that it was teetering around, say, 153. Since all your life you've weighed between 140 and 142, you'd know that you wanted to lose 10 pounds. But that's not all you'd know.

- You'd have a goal: To lose weight.
- The goal would be specific: 10 pounds.
- You'd have a time frame: Before my high school re-union, two months from now.

- You'd have a way to measure how you're doing: The scale.

And because you had that well-defined framework, you'd have a better chance of success—*much better* than if you were simply dieting with no goal and no end in sight.

You need to think of this quest—the quest to get out of debt and into wealth—in the same way. I know it's tempting to decide that you're going to get rid of every bit of your credit card debt this year, but you shouldn't aim that high. Why? Because you're not going to be able to do it. Most people in debt management programs run by credit counseling agencies take four to five years to emerge debt-free. They're also paying fees to the counselors for doing the work. You don't have to pay those fees. And although you may determine that you can't do this in less than four or five years (although if that happens, it's okay), I want you to try to do it in three. You'll still be breaking your big mountain of debt into smaller hills of debt that are actually possible to climb.

By doing this, you do yourself a great service. By giving yourself benchmarks that are actually achievable, you allow yourself to succeed. You'll feel great when you reach each one, and that will make you feel as if you can do even more. If instead you set out to grab the whole enchilada, not only will you feel terrible when you fail (as would likely happen), you won't give yourself the opportunity to do *better* than you anticipate. And that would be a shame.

So here's what your goal looks like broken down:

- You have a goal: Reduce debt.
- It's specific: By $10 a day.
- You have a time frame: Debt-free in three years.
- You have ways to measure how you're doing: Your balances (and, as we'll see in a little while, your credit score).

Question: So, what if I have more than $8,000 in debt? Answer: To knock off that debt in the same three-year period—which I like because it's not too short nor too long, and it gives you plenty of years to build wealth for the future—you have to free up more than $10 a day or decide that four or even five years to financial freedom is okay with you.

I know the numbers in my "Becoming Debt-Free" charts look discouraging, but I want you to pay very close attention to how much less painful this process

DEBT–FREE IN THREE YEARS

Rate →	12%	16%	18%	20%	24%
Debt					
$8,000	$9/day	$10/day	$10/day	$10/day	$11/day
$10,000	$11/day	$12/day	$12/day	$13/day	$13/day
$12,000	$13/day	$14/day	$15/day	$15/day	$16/day
$14,000	$16/day	$16/day	$17/day	$17/day	$18/day
$16,000	$18/day	$19/day	$19/day	$20/day	$21/day
$20,000	$22/day	$23/day	$24/day	$24/day	$26/day

DEBT–FREE IN FOUR YEARS

Rate →	12%	16%	18%	20%	24%
Debt					
$10,000	$9/day	$10/day	$10/day	$10/day	$11/day
$12,000	$11/day	$12/day	$12/day	$12/day	$13/day
$14,000	$12/day	$13/day	$14/day	$14/day	$15/day
$16,000	$14/day	$15/day	$16/day	$16/day	$17/day
$20,000	$18/day	$19/day	$20/day	$20/day	$22/day
$22,000	$21/day	$22/day	$22/day	$22/day	$23/day

DEBT–FREE IN FIVE YEARS

Rate →	12%	16%	18%	20%	24%
Debt					
$12,000	$9/day	$10/day	$10/day	$11/day	$12/day
$14,000	$11/day	$12/day	$12/day	$13/day	$14/day
$16,000	$12/day	$13/day	$14/day	$14/day	$16/day
$20,000	$15/day	$16/day	$17/day	$18/day	$19/day
$24,000	$18/day	$19/day	$20/day	$22/day	$23/day
$30,000	$23/day	$25/day	$25/day	$26/day	$29/day

is at lower interest rates. The key to being able to grab one of those lower rates is to manage a very important piece of information known as your credit score. We'll talk about that in the next chapter. Then we'll move on to finding the money you need to pay down those bills.

STEP 3

Know and Manage Your Credit Score

I F YOU'VE ever applied for any sort of credit—a credit card, cellular phone service, utility service such as gas or electric—then you have:

- a credit history,
- a credit report and
- a credit score.

How did this happen without you knowing about it? Why weren't you consulted?

Sorry, it doesn't work that way. When you went out and applied for your first loan or credit card, you filled out an application. The credit issuer called a credit bureau—probably one of the country's big three, TransUnion, Equifax or Experian—to check up on you, and that bureau, recognizing it didn't have any information on you, started a credit file.

The other bureaus learned about you just a short while later. Let's say the application you filled out was for a credit card. You signed the form, bought a few things and when the bill came, you paid it. Your credit card company closely monitored how you handled that transaction and sent details on you to all three bureaus, telling them whether you paid on time, what percentage of the outstanding debt you paid, and whether you stayed within your credit limit.

Voila! You had a credit history. It wasn't very deep or very detailed, but it existed, and each time you paid a bill you padded your file. As you added creditors, the file—and your credit report that is the written version of that file—grew thicker still. And although some information eventually falls off the report as it ages, much of it follows you around for as long as you have and manage credit—in other words, for the rest of your life.

Six months into your life as a borrower, there was enough information in your file for the credit bureaus to assign you something called a credit score. This is a numerical translation of that credit history that lenders (as well as insurers, employers, landlords and others) use to quickly make a decision about whether they want to do business with you—and about how much to charge if you ever want to do business with them. The score changes all the time as new information about you and your credit behavior is reported to each of the bureaus.

Credit scores, which look a lot like SAT (Scholastic Achievement Test) scores, range from about 350 (though it's rare to see one below 500) to more than 800 (equally rare). The vast majority of scores are produced by a California-based company named Fair Isaac and Co. Fair Isaac doesn't collect credit information—it's not a credit bureau—but it works with all three of the large credit bureaus to take the information they collect and turn it into credit or FICO (for Fair Isaac and Company) scores.

These scores pack a powerful punch. In 2003, 25 billion credit decisions were made based on FICO scores alone. These weren't just decisions about whether applicants would be approved for a new credit card; they also determined:

- How much the applicants could borrow
- What sort of interest rate they would pay
- Whether they qualified for an increase in their credit line
- Whether they qualified to rent an apartment
- Whether they could get a cell phone
- Whether they qualified for a cash advance
- Whether they would actually get the credit card they were "preapproved" for

Your credit history also determines:

- How much you'll have to pay for homeowners' and auto insurance; insurers have discovered that how and whether you pay your bills is more indicative of the number of claims you'll file than your driving record.
- Whether or not you'll get hired for a particular job. Employers aren't allowed to look at credit scores, but in situations in which you will be asked to handle a drawer of cash, they often look at credit reports for signs of financial trouble. They've learned it's not necessarily a good idea to put a person in front of a drawer of $20s when they have a stack of delinquent bills.

In other words, your score is a really powerful piece of information. And because it is a snapshot of your borrowing and bill-paying behavior over the previous 24 months, you have the power to change it for the better as time goes by. As you do that, you'll be able to swap some of your higher-rate credit card debts, mortgages and auto loans for lower rate ones, and that will enable you to pay back the money you owe both faster and cheaper.

So, I want you to check your credit score at the start of this process. You're not going to micromanage it, but after 12 months—or if you apply for a mortgage— you're going to check it again to see how you're doing.

The easiest (cheapest) way I know to do it is to go to the Web site we set up for this book—PayItDown.com— where the Fair Isaac folks have supplied us with a score simulator. You can also purchase an actual score at myfico.com.

What Can a Good Credit Score Do for You?

If you have a credit score of more than 620—and the vast majority of people do—you will be able to borrow more money. However, only when you get that score up past the 700—or even 720—mark will you be able to borrow that money at the very best prices.

This is a result of something called "risk-based pricing," a relatively new phenomenon in the lending industry. Back in the 1980s, everyone who had a credit card from Citibank, for example, paid the same rate. But as credit scoring technology improved, it became possible for Citibank to learn that Jane Doe was more likely to pay her bills on time than John Doe. So Citi— and the rest of the lenders in this country—decided that they'd fare better (in other words, keep their best customers happier *and* make more money) by rewarding Jane with a lower interest rate and penalizing Joe with a higher one. After all, Jane, who paid all her bills in full and on time, wasn't paying anything in interest anyway. That's why these days all lenders, not just credit card companies, use some form of risk-based pricing.

The score that *you* need to get that best price (or at least not the worst one) varies by the product you're shopping for.

Your mortgage and your score. The score you need to qualify for a plain-vanilla 30-year fixed-rate mortgage is 620. That qualifies you for a mortgage that Fannie Mae and Freddie Mac will purchase in the secondary market. But that 620 isn't going to buy you a very good interest rate. As you'll see in the chart that follows, even small improvements in your score can mean a huge savings in your mortgage. Improving your score by 100 points from 620 to 720 can mean an extra $90,000 in your pocket over the life of your loan.

Let's say you're borrowing $200,000 to buy a house. With the prime rate at 4 percent in January 2004, the chart below shows you what that loan would have cost you—on average—based on your credit score:

COST OF $200,000 LOAN			
Score	*Interest Rate*	*Monthly Payment*	*Total Interest Paid Over 30 Years*
720–850	5.501%	$1,136	$208,853
700–719	5.626%	$1,151	$214,518
675–699	6.163%	$1,220	$239,250
620–674	7.313%	$1,373	$294,247
560–619	8.531%	$1,542	$355,200
500–559	9.289%	$1,651	$394,362

Your auto loan and your score. Auto lenders are completely aware that bringing in a customer with a score of, say, 640 is significantly better than bringing in a customer with a score of 600. They have detailed models that tell them that 640 borrowers are *half* as likely to default on their loans. And the prices reflect that: on a $20,000 car loan in January 2004, a customer with a 640 score would save $2,000 in interest over the life of a 60-month loan, as shown in the chart below.

Your credit cards and your score. In general, the credit

COST OF $20,000 LOAN			
Score	**Interest Rate**	**Monthly Payment**	**Total Interest Paid Over 30 Years**
720–850	4.931%	$460	$2,078
700–719	5.659%	$467	$2,396
675–699	7.894%	$487	$3,389
620–674	10.808%	$515	$4,722
560–619	15.126%	$558	$6,779
500–559	18.530%	$593	$8,467

card industry works the same way: the higher your score, the lower your interest rate. There really is no credit score—not even 500—at which you can't qualify for a credit card. The bank may ask you to deposit some money to secure the credit until you prove (after 18 or 24 months) that you'll pay your bills. But you can still get one.

Interestingly, you can get to the point where a credit card issuer thinks your score is too high. In a credit card issuer's world, a score of 720 or 730 is optimal; 800 is too high. How is that possible? There's a correlation between credit inactivity and a very high score. People who use a credit card rarely or only in case of an emergency represent more of a cost than a benefit to credit card companies. Such people rarely pay their bills late—and they certainly aren't very risky—but card companies still have to send them a statement once a month and still have to send them literature when they make a change in the credit card program. If you're this sort of person, the card company may eventually decide they don't want to do business with you.

How Can You Increase Your Score?

There are a number of ways you can improve your score. For example, while it sounds like a no-brainer, you should be consistent about using your name. Use the same one all the time: first, middle (if you're including one) and last, as well as any Jrs. or IIIs. If you hyphenate, hyphenate with regularity. If you've decided to take your maiden name as your middle name, make it legal. That way, the credit bureaus are less likely to confuse your information with that of someone else. Beyond that, you can improve your score by taking a look at how it is computed—and knowing what you need to do to improve in each area.

Thirty-five percent of your score is based upon how well you pay your bills.

How to boost your score: Start paying on time. If you make late payments, the amount your score will suffer depends on how late and how frequent your delinquencies are. One 30- or 60-day late payment is a lot less damaging than 15 late payments during the last 15 years. It also matters how recently these episodes occurred. A single incident five months ago still counts. A single incident five years ago no longer matters. For example, one late payment in the recent past could lower your score 20 points. (One that's currently late, and still unpaid, could drop it **double** that.) A pattern of late payments could lower your score 50 or 60 points.

Thirty percent of your score is what Fair Isaac calls "balance and burden," a measure of how much credit you have available to you and how much of that credit you're using.

How to boost your score: You're in the best shape if you're using 20 to 30 percent of the credit available to you. But the way to get to that level is not by canceling and cutting up all your credit cards. I know that's what you've been told to do, but the people telling you that are wrong.

I'm not saying you'll never cancel a credit card. You may decide, as you go through the Pay It Down program, that you need to lighten up on the plastic in your wallet. You just need to understand that in the short term, canceling cards will have a negative impact on your score. Why? Think of the percentage of credit you're using now—your credit utilization—as a fraction:

$$\frac{\text{Credit you're using}}{\text{Credit available to you}} \quad = \quad \text{Credit utilization}$$

Say you have 10 cards and each of those has a $1,000 limit. You have $10,000 in revolving credit available to you. Now suppose you're only using five of your cards and that those five cards are all maxed out. You're using half of the credit available to you, which puts your credit utilization at 50 percent:

$$\frac{\$5,000}{\$10,000} \quad = \quad 50\%$$

If you decide you don't need all of those cards—that you're going to tidy up your wallet and close the five you're not using—you dramatically reduce the credit you have available to you. Now you're using *all* of the credit you have available, which puts your credit utilization at 100 percent:

$$\frac{\$5,000}{\$5,000} \quad = \quad 100\%$$

This level of utilization could send your score down by 100 points.

Now, that doesn't mean you should *never* cancel credit cards. If you have been struggling to get out of credit card debt and you've made progress, and you don't want to be tempted to dig yourself back in— then by all means, cancel the cards. You would be sacrificing your score in the short term for much longer-term financial well-being. What you should *not* do, however, is cancel cards right before you apply for a mortgage, auto loan, or other big loan. Instead, lock your cards away where you won't be tempted to touch them. After you get your mortgage or auto loan, then call and cancel. As you make progress paying down the other credit cards in your wallet, your ratio will come back in line and your score will rise.

(*Note*: Don't worry that paying off your balances every month is a bad thing—it isn't. By the time you receive your bill, write your check and mail it in, and it's cashed, posted and reported to the credit bureaus, you've already gotten the bill for the next month. In other words, if you're making frequent use of your card, you never show a zero balance to the bureaus.)

Ten percent is based on your search for new credit—how recently you have opened (or inquired about opening) new accounts.

How to boost your score: Today, the smart shopper doesn't just walk into the local bank and apply for a mortgage. She shops around for the best rate, going on-line to see what sorts of deals are available, calling a local mortgage broker, and perhaps applying at that local bank where they might give her a preferential rate because she's been a good customer for years. Along the way, it wouldn't be unusual for 10 or 15 different institutions to check her credit score. Her credit score won't be in jeopardy if she shops around in that way. Auto- or mortgage-related inquiries (resulting in a score being pulled by the auto or mortgage lender) that occur within 14 days of each other simply say to the credit bureau that you're shopping for a car or a house, and they're counted as one inquiry. Any inquiries older than 12 months don't count at all.

When a credit card company pulls your report, however, it's another story. A single application for a single card isn't a sign of trouble, but multiple card inquiries are a sign that you need money. Generally, that's not good. Multiple inquiries, particularly if you've had credit for only a few years, can mean a loss of 50 to 100 points on your score.

(*Note:* This means that when you hit the mall, it's not a good idea to accept every offer for instant credit—even if it means you're going to get 10 percent off the cost of your purchase. I understand the offers are compelling. I also understand that it's been a long time since the salesclerk hasn't asked you if you want to "save 10 percent." I know that some of those salesclerks will even advise you to simply close the account if you don't want it after you get home. Closing the account, however, won't stop the inquiry from damaging your credit rating. So bide your time. Save the 10 percent offer for when you're buying a $2,700 couch, not a $27 handbag.)

Ten percent is the financial composition of your file: what percentage is bank–card debt and what percentage is installment debt?

How to boost your score: In the world of credit scoring, balance is important. It's better to have a ratio of 60 to 70 percent bank–card debt to 30 to 40 percent installment debt than to have too much more of one or the other. If your ratios are out of whack, you can use these guidelines to help you pay back one lender or another. But don't obsess over this component. It's the hardest element to control and represents a relatively small portion of your score.

Fifteen percent is a measure of the length of your credit relationships: How long have you had the cards in your wallet?

How to boost your score: If and when you decide to cancel your credit cards, try not to cancel the ones you've had the longest. It's good to have at least one card in your wallet that's more than two years old. Once you've had a card for 15 to 20 years, it won't send your score any higher.

You'll be surprised at how quickly the changes you make can boost your score. It's quite possible to see an increase of 25 points inside of a year, according to the folks at Fair Isaac.

When might you *not* see that kind of a boost? Increasing your score will be more difficult if you have a bankruptcy in your history or more than one 90–day–late payment. At that point, you're going to have to keep your behavior in check for the next couple of years while simultaneously following the foregoing advice. In other words, *wait it out.* Your score can improve as negative information moves toward the back—or, better yet, falls off your report. Credit scores are built to *predict* what will happen over the next 24 months: how likely it is that you'll fall behind in your payments over the next 24 months. For that reason, it makes the most sense—analytically—to the lender to weigh most heavily your behavior over the *previous* 24 months. So negative information counts less after it's over 24 months old. Unfortunately, even if you've cleaned up bad behavior, it takes time for negative information to vanish completely. Although some states have legislated this on their own—in New York, for example, negative information can stay on your report only five years—most of the country sticks to this schedule:

- Late payments: 7 years
- Debt management plan (through credit counselor): 7 years
- Chapter 13 bankruptcy: 7 years
- Chapter 7 bankruptcy: 10 years

What should you do with all of this information? Use it to guide your behavior over the next 12 months and beyond. Of course, you're not going to wait until your credit score has improved to start putting aside your $10 a day and using it to your advantage. But as your scores improve, you'll be able to manage your interest rates as well—swapping your high-rate cards for lower-rate ones and getting your Visa issuer to give you a break with a simple phone call. As I said, that's a few months down the road. Right now, it's time to come up with some cash.

Tales of Life and Debt:
Recovering from a Lousy Credit Score, Dollar by Dollar

Back in the fall of 2001, Lydia and Brian, a two-career couple in Washington, D.C., decided they wanted to build a house. They found a builder they wanted to work with, a subdivision in suburban Maryland in which they wanted to live and—excited at the prospects—went about prequalifying for a mortgage. All of a sudden, their bubble burst.

Mortgage rates at the time were near historic lows. Lydia and Brian were counting on using those rates to help them buy a house big enough to grow into. But their potential lender told them they would be able to qualify only for rates two to three percentage points higher. Why? Lousy credit scores—between 580 and 620, to be more precise.

"We knew we had six to nine months before the home was ready—we were building from the ground up," explains Lydia. "So we decided to take the time to work on improving our credit scores and our overall financial situation."

The first thing they needed to know was what, precisely, was dragging their scores down. They pulled both their credit scores and their credit reports. Without too much detection work, they found the culprits. "One reason our credit scores were so low was that there was a lot of outdated information on our credit reports," Lydia explains. Accounts had been closed. Late payments that had occurred more than seven years earlier should have already dropped off the report. Lydia and Brian took matters into their own hands, sending certified letters to all three credit reports disputing the information and noting, specifically, which items should be updated and which should be removed. "It took us some time to clean up those credit reports," Lydia recalls. "I also called or wrote to the various creditors to make sure they updated their records."

The other reason for the couple's low scores was hidden in their bulging wallets: 12 credit cards, each used to 50 percent of its limit—or more. That made the couple's debt–to–income ratio—an important component of their credit scores—higher than it should be. No amount of letter writing, even certified letter writing, could take care of that. Instead, Lydia and Brian had to hunker down.

They decided to forgo eating out as much as possible. They cut back the money they were spending on clothing and travel. They began to dump every available penny into a money–market account, which they then used to pay off their credit cards. Over the next nine months, they paid off 11 of 12 credit cards—and, to eliminate temptation, closed 7 of them. They then stopped using credit cards completely and saved an additional $10,000 to put down on their home.

When they went back to their lender several weeks before they closed on the house, he was astonished to see the difference in their credit scores. They had jumped to between 650 and 730 points. The result: Lydia and Brian qualified for a three–year adjustable–rate mortgage at 4.95 percent. With their old scores the rate could have gone as high as 7 percent; their nine–month exercise in frugality saved them $400 a month on their mortgage payment—nearly $5,000 a year.

To this day, Lydia and Brian pull their credit scores

every six months to make sure they've remained high, an exercise that has continued to pay off. In August 2003, they refinanced their mortgage at a fixed 5.75 percent for 30 years. At that time, their home was appraised at $100,000 higher than its original appraisal. "I am an example of a person who learned how to repay her debts," says Lydia, proud of her achievements. It wasn't easy, but she did it—step by step, dollar by dollar. Without professional help.

STEP 4

Track Your Spending

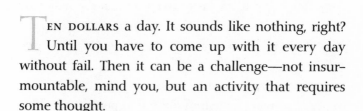

TEN DOLLARS a day. It sounds like nothing, right? Until you have to come up with it every day without fail. Then it can be a challenge—not insurmountable, mind you, but an activity that requires some thought.

It also requires—and though this may sound like a no-brainer, for many people it's anything but—that you know where your money is going. Most people don't. In fact, many people also don't fully comprehend the fact that they're spending more than they bring in each month. For my last book, *You Don't Have to Be Rich: Comfort, Happiness and Financial Security on Your Own Terms*, published in 2003, the polling folks at

RoperASW did a big piece of research. From it we learned that:

- Eighty-five percent of people believe that no matter how much or how little money they make, they'll be able to live on it.
- Half of those people don't pay off their credit card bills each month.
- Half of *those* people don't save anything.

What does that mean? To me, it means that we've forgotten what it means to live on what we make. By not paying off our credit cards, we're living on borrowed money. By not saving, we're living on borrowed time.

It was very, very different in our parents' day. Their generation was hardwired to save 10 percent of whatever they earned for a rainy day. If and when they had an emergency—whether it was a small one (the transmission dying) or a big one (a health scare)—they were able to draw on those savings. They didn't have to worry (at least for a little while) that they'd lose their homes or fall deep into debt.

But we don't have that kind of safety net. We may earn a decent living—in many families we earn two—

but we spend as much as we earn on our mortgages, car loans, day care and other "fixed" expenses. When an emergency hits, we don't have the savings our parents had to draw on. If we lose a job, suffer an illness or have to take a break from the workforce to care for a child who's having trouble in school or a parent who's getting on in years, our finances simply can't handle it. You hear people time and time again talking about "the fragile middle class." This lack of a safety net—of savings—is what makes us so fragile.

How do we turn the situation around? The *only* way to do it is to start living within our means and saving a little something . . . just in case. The only way to do that is to know:

- What's coming in,
- What's going out and
- Where it's going.

What's Coming In

Do you know how much money you'll earn this year—before *and* after taxes? That after-tax number is the key. Mentally budgeting to live on your gross, or pretax, income is a guarantee you'll overspend. Say you're a single person earning a gross salary of $48,000 a year, a very decent number. If you plan on spending anywhere near that $48,000, you've overdone it, because even if you live in a state that doesn't raid the pot, Uncle Sam is going to take a $6,900 cut. And you'll end up $6,900 in the hole.

So stop and take a look at how much you're bringing in before and after taxes. Use the chart that follows to record your information. If you receive a regular paycheck, this information is on your pay stub. If you work for yourself and business has been pretty consistent, then use last year's earnings as a guide. Use last year's number even if you think you're going to earn more this year; being conservative is insurance that you won't spend more than you actually bring in. Write down your earnings number. Apply your tax rate. The resulting difference is what you're working with. Divide this by 12. That's your monthly take-home pay.

Your annual pretax income: $_____

Your annual after-tax income: $_____

Your monthly after-tax income: $_____

What's Going Out

You have two different types of expenses: fixed and variable. Your fixed costs represent the money you've already agreed to spend each month. Think of them as things you need, things that are nonnegotiable and indispensable. (In reality, many of them are likely *very* negotiable and *quite* dispensable. We'll come back to that in a minute.)

The chart that follows includes items that you pay quarterly or semiannually, such as home and auto insurance. In recording your expenses, divide your payments into monthly increments to get an accurate assessment of what it's costing you each month. And, since we're dealing with fixed costs, use just the minimum you're required to pay each month on your credit cards here.

Your fixed expenses

Rent/mortgage $_____

Common charges (condo fees, etc.) $_____

Car payment 1 $_____

Car payment 2 $_____

Car payment 3 $_____

Train ticket or other
    commuting expenses $_____

Child support $_____

Alimony $_____

Back taxes $_____

Parking expenses $_____

Student loan payment $_____

Credit card payment $_____

Electric $_____

Gas $_____

Oil $_____

Water $_____

Other utilities $_____

Health club $_____

Internet $_____

Phone (landline) $_____

Phone (cellular) $_____

Wireless device (PDA) $_____

Child care/baby–sitter $_____

Health insurance $_____

Homeowners insurance $_____

Auto insurance $_____

Life insurance $_____

Regular prescriptions $_____

Payments for other purchases
   (furniture, appliances, etc.) $_____

Housekeeper $_____

Lawn care $_____

College tuition $_____

Private school $_____

Tutoring $_____

After–school programs $_____

Sports for the kids $_____

Summer camp	$_____
Other	$_____
Fixed expenses monthly total	$_____

Once you add the numbers up, you'll be able to see the difference between what you make each month and what you've *already agreed* to spend each month. If you're surprisingly close to the line—or over it—you're not the only one. For many, many people (particularly those in big cities), housing alone eats up 50 percent of what they take home each month. That immediately sets them up to fail. But although you may perceive these expenses to be "fixed," they're not really. There are ways that you can cut almost every one. But before we do that, you need to know how much you're spending in areas that aren't fixed as well.

Where's the Rest of Your Money Going?

Even if you have some wiggle room in the fixed categories, you may still feel like you're strangled with debt and unable to save. That may be because you're spending too much on other things.

I'll bet, however, that if I asked you how much you spend on these variable items, you'd have absolutely no idea. That's because the amounts vary from month to month. It's also because few of us keep track of where our cash goes. We head to the ATM, withdraw $50 or $100, spend it randomly and withdraw another chunk of cash when the money's gone. Keeping track is too time-consuming, too detail-oriented, so most of us simply don't bother. But while you're going through this makeover, you have to. The only way to get a realistic idea of what you're spending your money on is to track it.

So, I want you to get a little notebook, one small enough to fit in your pocket or your purse. Slide a pen through the spirals (there will be no "but I didn't have a pen" excuses for not writing things down). Starting today, I want you to write down everything you spend. *Everything.* You may not think it matters that you drop 75 cents a day into the soda machine at work, but that 75 cents is $16.25 a month and $195 a year. In other words, it's a plane ticket, a car payment— *it's real money.*

When you get home each night, categorize those expenses on a legal pad. Keep running totals for a month of how much you're spending on:

Your variable expenses

Groceries $\underline{\hspace{3cm}}$

Restaurant meals $\underline{\hspace{3cm}}$

Takeout breakfast $\underline{\hspace{3cm}}$

Takeout lunch $\underline{\hspace{3cm}}$

Takeout dinner $\underline{\hspace{3cm}}$

Coffee $\underline{\hspace{3cm}}$

Snacks $\underline{\hspace{3cm}}$

Gasoline $\underline{\hspace{3cm}}$

Clothing, shoes, accessories $\underline{\hspace{3cm}}$

Entertaining
   (dinner parties, cocktail parties) $\underline{\hspace{3cm}}$

Entertainment
   (movies, theater tickets,
   sporting events) $\underline{\hspace{3cm}}$

Dry cleaning $\underline{\hspace{3cm}}$

Cards $\underline{\hspace{3cm}}$

Gifts (and gift wrap) $\underline{\hspace{3cm}}$

Newspapers and magazines $_____

Books $_____

CDs/music $_____

Videos/DVDs $_____

Things for the house
(sheets, towels, kitchen
accessories, decorating) $_____

Wine, beer, liquor $_____

Cigarettes $_____

Drug–store expenses
(shampoo, nonprescription
medications) $_____

Other medical expenses
(appointments, services that
aren't reimbursed) $_____

Grooming expenses
(manicures, haircuts) $_____

Pet food $_____

Pet grooming $_____

Veterinary bills $_____

Other $_____

**Variable expenses
    monthly total** $_____

Okay, so now it's time to see where you stand. First, get a total of how much you're spending each month:

Monthly total fixed expenses $_____

+ Monthly total variable expenses $_____

= Monthly total all expenses $_____

Now, let's see whether you're exceeding your income.

Monthly after-tax income $_____

– Monthly total all expenses $_____

**= Your monthly profit
    (savings) or loss** $_____

How'd you do? When you add together your fixed and variable expenses, are you still in positive territory? If you are, then you are essentially living on what you make. That doesn't mean there's no room for improvement; by spending less, you can save more and pay down your existing debts faster. That will mean more money in your pocket and less padding of the accounts of your credit card companies—and that will help you get a lock on your financial future.

If you're not in positive territory—or if you're so close there's no wiggle room—you're spending too much. It's time to turn that equation around, to get you out of the red and into the black, and on the road to personal profitability.

Tales of Life and Debt:
"We Didn't Know How Much We Spent!"

"I wasn't very well educated in the world of money," says Al, a project manager for a telecommunications company in Atlanta. "And that made it one of the most difficult topics for me to talk about. I never asked my parents how much they made. They never sat me down to go over what a budget is. One day after I graduated from college and started making money and spending money, my father sat me down and asked where my money was going. I said, 'Hey, Dad. Did you earn this money? No. Then don't ask me.'"

Al probably would have been better off if he'd had that conversation with his father no matter how uncomfortable it made him. As it was, it took him a good decade to figure out precisely where his money was going—and that sabotaged his ability to save as much as possible for everything from college to retirement.

Al and his wife, Jean, have been married for 20 years. At the beginning of their life together, he went to work, and she handled the at-home budgeting—a very traditional division of labor. But over the years, Al realized that although he knew how much he was bringing home in each paycheck (and roughly how much Jean was taking in from her part-time job), he had very little idea where they were spending all that money.

That was just the beginning of their downward spiral. Although neither Al nor his wife were raised with credit cards, both developed an affinity for charging. They convinced themselves they were spending money on things they needed. Al would walk into a department store and blow $1,400 on four suits he needed for work. Together, they wouldn't think twice about charging a $150 dinner on a weekend, then spending another $30 at the movies.

They lived this sort of free-spending life for years. Then one day they realized that the balances on their combined cards had hit $20,000. They had no money in the bank and no retirement savings to speak of. Jean panicked. "She was worrying continuously for about six months," Al said. He took a step back and decided panicking wasn't going to do them any good. "I said, 'This is crazy. We just have to stop charging. We need to put the cards away and be disciplined.'"

The next week he picked up a copy of Quicken, the popular personal finance software. Quicken—though it does many other more sophisticated tasks as well— is, at its core, an electronic check register. You input how much you spend on which specific items; it deducts the expenditures from your overall balance. Whenever you'd like to know how much you're spending category by category, you can simply push a button and see your spending habits in pie-chart form.

Al was amazed. "When you're just looking at the individual numbers, the individual expenses, you really have no idea what you're spending your money on. I was amazed at how much we spent on groceries, how much we spent on our cars. When you're just looking at your balance, you're not thinking ahead about where you want your money to go." But that's what Quicken forced him to do. It forced him to start choosing where his money might do him the most good.

And over the past few years, making those choices has enabled Al and Jean to dig their way out of debt. They stopped eating out as frequently, stopped spending money on cars and clothes. It took two and a half years for them to clear the $20,000 in credit card debt. But they didn't stop there. They started overpaying on their car loan, tacking on another $150 to the $350 they owed each month. The result: They shaved a year and a half off the term of the loan. They're overpaying on their mortgage as well, aiming to have the house paid in full in the next five years. The credit cards in their lives have been replaced by debit cards—although they have continued to hold off on big expenses. (Al would like a new car to replace his second one, a nine-year-old Honda, but he says. "I just don't want to cut the check for a new car. I want to write a check to the mutual fund for that amount.") And they're saving. "We still don't have a full three months' emergency savings," Al acknowledges. "But we have something."

Al sums it up: "By the time I'm 50, I want to know that my house is paid off. I want to know I have money in the bank. I don't want the stress of owing money to other people. I want my balance sheet to be absolutely clean."

STEP 5

Find the Money

D ID YOU ever see the movie *Dave*? In it, Kevin Kline played a look–alike for the president of the United States who takes over the job when the real president has a stroke while fooling around with his secretary. (Yes, it's a comedy.) In one scene Dave is faced with shutting down a day–care center for under-privileged kids—unless he can find some wiggle room in the government's budget. So he brings his home-town CPA (Charles Grodin) to the White House and they sit around the kitchen table at midnight, chowing down and figuring out where they can make cuts. They get creative. And they succeed.

And that's precisely what you need to do.

Before we dive in, though, you need to agree that you'll be willing to make some hard choices about spending money on particular items. Let's take your cell phone as an example. If you're like many people, you've come to rely very heavily on your cell phone. You may have started using it for convenience, or only in emergencies, but over the last few years, it's become the easiest and best way to reach you. You can't imagine giving it up. Or could you? Analysts say the average cell phone bill is $54 a month. That's $648 a year. Could you give it up—or use it substantially less often—if that was what you needed to do to come up with your $10 a day? How about your high-speed Internet access? Or your second car? Or that second dinner out each week?

These are hard questions. And no one can answer them for you. The problem is that if you're not balancing your budget already, you may not be able to do it by getting rid of the small expenditures (like the lattes you allow yourself every so often). You may have to eliminate or trim some bigger line items.

I'll make you a deal: I'll go through this process in an order designed to cause you the least amount of pain, one that will ask you to give up the fewest number of things in life that you enjoy. But once you've found your $10 a day, it's up to you; you can stop, knowing that you've succeeded (and it's a success that should be celebrated!), or you can keep reading and determine if there's a way for you to more quickly build a savings cushion, or a larger nest egg. Or you can use the excess to save for other goals you might have in mind.

For example...

What could you do with an extra $50 a month?
   Replace your decrepit dishwasher
   Join a gym

What could you do with an extra $100 a month?
   Buy season tickets to your favorite sports team's games
   Take your family on a weeklong vacation

What could you do with an extra $200 a month?
   Pay for your newborn child's wedding
   Send your teenager to sleep-away camp for a month

What could you do with an extra $500 a month?
   Put a two-year-old through college in 16 years
   Put a down payment on a home in 5 years

So let's go through the process. At the end of each step, I want you to keep a running total of how much money you were able to find.

Find the Money: Change Your Withholding

Did you get a tax refund last year? Do you seem to get one every year? You may love the thought of getting a nice fat check to brighten up each winter, but you should *not* be giving Uncle Sam an interest-free loan (if the shoe were on the other foot, the government wouldn't give one to you). Plus, the money would serve you better if you were getting it in consistent pieces throughout the year.

How much would changing your withholding put in *your* pocket?

Found Money: $_____/month

(*Reader*: You'll find these total lines throughout the book. Use them to keep track of how much you're able to free up each month. And don't worry ... there are a lot of these blanks to come. You'll find even small amounts can quickly add up.)

Find the Money: Reduce Your Interest Rates

When you take a look at the expenses listed in the previous section, you'll notice many of them are borrowing costs:

- Mortgage
- Home equity loan or line of credit
- Car loan
- Student loan
- Credit card payments

From the late 1990s through the first part of the twenty-first century, we've been fortunate to enjoy some of the lowest interest rates in history. At the same time, the values of our homes have appreciated quite rapidly. Those two things combined have allowed us to refinance our home mortgages and at the same time pull out some of that appreciated equity, or pull out some of that equity using a home equity line of credit.

Now that sounds really good on the surface: we pull money out of our homes that we agree to pay back over the next 30 years at a very attractive rate. The interest is deductible to boot, which takes that very attractive rate and turns it into one that's extremely attractive. Then we use that money to pay off higher-rate debts: our credit cards and our car loans. The quality of our personal balance sheet improves tremendously. So does our cash flow.

But that's theory. In practice, it's not all that neat and tidy. What happens to many people who use consolidation loans to pay down high-rate credit card debt is that they charge those credit cards right back up again. In fact, some new research from Matthew Greenwald and Associates showed that a full one-third of people who took out consolidation loans had regenerated significant credit card debt a scant four years later. That means they're even more strapped than they were before. And because they've turned an unsecured debt (those credit card bills) into secured debt (a bigger mortgage or home equity loan), they've put their homes on the line. If the end result of all this is that they're unable to pay their mortgage and home equity loan bills, the bank can take their homes.

(*Note:* I'm not suggesting that turning high-rate credit card and car loan debt into low-rate mortgage debt is a bad idea for everyone. I'm suggesting you must know yourself, your habits, your strengths and your weaknesses *before* you do it. You must be sure that you're not going to charge your credit cards up again. If you're at all uncertain that you have the fortitude to stick by your guns, you should either put safeguards in place—get rid of your credit cards and use only debit cards, or write checks and use cash—or don't do the deal at all.)

The better way to approach reducing your interest rates is to see if—and how—you can significantly cut your borrowing costs *without* putting your home on the line. So, before we even consider debt consolidation, we'll look at how much you can save by bringing down your interest rates on your other debts: your credit cards, car loans, student loans and personal loans. We'll look at refinancing your mortgage without pulling out additional cash. If, at the end of the day, a cash-out refinance or home equity line/loan is the only way to make ends meet, you can proceed, with caution.

Find the Money: Cut Your Credit Card Interest

Cutting your credit card interest rate is really just a matter of doing one of two things: reducing the rates on your current cards or transferring your balances to cheaper cards. In order to do either, you need to know where you stand. Start by laying all your cards out on the table and listing the APR (annual percentage rate; or interest rate) you're paying on each. Note whether those rates are fixed or variable. Next, ready your ammunition. Gather all the preapproved offers you've received in the mail. (When you call your companies to ask for a break, you need to be able to tell them who's offering you a better deal and how much better it is.) And have a rough idea of how valuable a customer you've been: how long you have had the card, how much you charge a month or year, how much interest they're earning each year on your business, and whether you pay on time. When you've got it together, you can proceed.

• *Call the toll-free customer service number and ask for a lower rate.* A 2002 U.S. Public Interest Research Group (PIRG) study showed that calling and asking for a lower rate results in a reduction 56 percent of the time—and a substantial reduction at that. Customers got an average break of one-third off the current interest rate. Here's a script to follow when you call. Begin with:

> *"I have [name of card] with you and my interest rate is [X] percent. I received another offer in the mail from [other*

bank's name] for [X] percent, but before I take it, I want to see if you can lower my interest rate instead."

If the representative says they're not authorized to do that, you say:

"Look, you and I both know that if I transfer my balance today, next week your bank is going to send me an offer to come back at an even lower rate. Why don't you just save the bank the cost of that effort by giving me several points today?"

If the rep says it's not possible because your credit card is at a fixed interest rate, you say:

"Actually, that doesn't have anything to do with whether or not you have the ability to lower my interest rate. A fixed interest rate only means that my rate doesn't vary with fluctuations in the prime rate. In fact, the bank can raise it on my account at any time by just giving me 15 days' written notice. And the bank can—if it chooses— lower the rate today."

If the rep still says they're not authorized to do that, you say:

"I'd like to speak to your supervisor."

• *Speak to a supervisor and ask again.* Even if you get a substantial cut in the interest rate from the first person, it's worth speaking to a supervisor to see if you can do any better. The person on the front line of customer service will be authorized only to cut your rate by a preset amount (if at all). The customer service representative may also insist that the supervisor doesn't have the power to cut your rate either, or—if you've already gotten a break—to cut it further. That may not be true, so insist on speaking to the supervisor anyway.

• *Threaten to close your account.* Let me be clear here: You don't *want* to close your account. It won't do good things to your credit score. However, if the bank believes that you're willing to close your account—and you've been a profitable customer—then you stand a better chance of getting what you want.

• *Keep a record of whom you spoke to and what was said.* If your promised rate cut—or fee waiver—doesn't materialize, then you're going to need a paper trail to back up your story. Knowing to whom you spoke, when the call was placed and what was promised is key.

• *Transfer your balance.* If you're not successful in reducing your interest rate over the phone, it's time to transfer your balance. There are two places to find good balance transfer offers: your mailbox (the average person gets five credit card solicitations a month) and at Web sites, including bankrate.com and cardweb.com.

Once you've decided its time to transfer your balance to another card, be sure to consider the following:

• *The rate.* Balance transfer offers often come with teaser rates—i.e., low rates for the first 6 or 12 months that then shoot sky high. You're going to be paying off your highest-rate debts first (more about that in step 9 "Pay It Down—Intelligently"), but that really means that the teaser puts the brakes on the new interest you're accruing on that preexisting debt. For that reason, the rate *after* the teaser expires is just as important (if not more so) than the teaser itself.

• *The fine print.* Balance transfers often incur different interest rates from those for new purchases. Cash advances sometimes have a third rate. It's important to understand at the outset what all of those rates are. It's also important to understand what "preapproved" does and doesn't mean. You may get an offer in the mail that says you're preapproved for a particular card, but while the interest rate in large print looks tempting, you must keep reading. The rest of the text will likely alert you to the fact that the company is using tiered pricing. This means it offers a range of interest rates—from the lowest of the low to the highest of the high—and you will be assigned an APR based on your credit history. The bottom line: You may not be getting the deal you think you are.

• *The fees.* Some card issuers charge a fee for balance transfers. Generally it's a percentage—sometimes capped—of the amount you're moving. The key is to know how much that will cost you before you make your move.

Heads up! Now that you've worked so hard to reduce your credit card interest rate, you need to know that there's only one way to keep it down: **pay on time.** Late payment fees have soared to an average $35 a pop, but more than that, a single late payment to your credit card company can trigger an interest rate hike as high as 29 percent. According to U.S. PIRG, two-thirds of banks raise rates after a single late payment. And what qualifies as "late" has gotten earlier and earlier. Most major card companies now consider a payment late if it arrives after 2 P.M. on the date it is due, and the due date is often only days after you receive your bill. One way to make sure your payments

How to Compare Credit Card Offers

If you've been offered one credit card you've been offered a dozen. How do you know which one to take? The key is in the box—the Schumer Box, that is. Every credit card solicitation now has to have a disclosure chart (called a Schumer Box after Senator Charles Schumer from New York, who pushed for it). Line your offers up side by side and compare the following information that each box includes:

- The actual APR (after the introductory/teaser period; the lower the better)
- The formula for computing a variable APR
- The length of the grace period (the longer the better; look for 25 days or more)
- The annual fee (most cards these days, except for mileage and platinum cards, don't have one)
- The minimum finance charge
- The transaction fees (for cash advances, balance transfers, etc.)
- The method used for computing your balance ("adjusted balance" is best for consumers but is rare; "average daily balance," a good second choice for consumers, is the most common; "two-cycle balance" is not good for consumers and should be avoided)
- The fees charged for paying late and going over your credit limit

arrive on time is to switch to on–line bill payment. You can schedule payments in advance and know without a doubt that your money will get there on time.

Found Money: $_____/month

Find the Money: Refinance Your Car Loan

Not everyone knows this, but you *can* refinance your car loan. In fact, it's much easier than refinancing your mortgage. Why? There is no appraisal process, for one thing. The fees—if any—are minimal. (You may have to pay $5 to $10 to your state's department of motor vehicles to get a new car title.)

Can you benefit?

- Yes, if you didn't shop well in the first place. If you financed through a dealer within the last few years (and have decent credit), you likely got a rate in the 8 to 10 percent range. You can do better.
- Yes, if you still owe a sizable amount. Most lenders require a car to be less than five years old and have a minimum balance of $7,500 in order to refinance.

- Yes, if you're not "upside down." Your car is collateral, so many lenders won't underwrite a car that's not worth the amount you owe on the loan.
- Yes, if your credit has improved. If you bought the car when your credit was blemished (or when you had little credit history at all) and you've cleaned up your act, refinancing can mean a significant drop in rates.

So what do you do next?

First, know what your car is worth. You can pull a value out of the Kelley Blue Book on the Web at kbb.com. As long as it's worth more than you owe, you're in good shape. If not, promise yourself you won't unload this car until you've righted this equation—or better yet, have paid it off entirely.

Second, shop around. The best car loan deals typically come from on-line lenders and credit unions. To find the best rates, head to bankrate.com, where a nifty search engine can pinpoint the best rates nationally and in your area. If you belong to a credit union, call them as well. If you don't belong to a credit union but would like to join (a good idea, as credit unions often have the best saving rates as well as the lowest lending rates), go to cuna.org (the Web site of the Credit Union National Association) for a list of institutions that might be willing to accept you as a member.

Third, apply for a loan. When you find what you think the best rate is for you, don't hesitate—just go for it. There's very little downside to this. The one thing you *don't* want to do is extend the term of your loan. If you do this, then decide you want out before you're done paying it off, you run the risk of being upside down (owing more than it's worth). That's how you dig into a deeper debt hole. Most lenders will happily match the term that already exists on your loan, even if it's be–tween their normal terms of 36, 48 and 60 months.

Fourth, reap the savings. Take a $25,000 48–month car loan for example:

Original interest rate: 8 percent.
Your original monthly payment: $622
New interest rate: 5.4 percent
New monthly payment: $580
Monthly savings: $42
Total savings: $2,016

Found Money: $_____/month

Find the Money: Consolidate Your Student Loans

Consolidating your student loans is another no–cost option that could free up considerable cash. Interest rates on federal student loans are near their lowest levels in history. If you took out your student loans (most people have more than one) when those rates were significantly higher, you have a single opportunity to roll all of those loans into one (which means a single monthly payment—hooray!) at a lower interest rate. The other benefit of consolidating is that you lock in that rate. When you took out your loans, they were variable–rate loans; when you consolidate, you move to a fixed–rate product.

How do you do it? First, get a grip on your balance. If all of your loans are through a single lender, you have no choice but to consolidate with that lender, but if you got your loans through more than one source, you're not locked into working with them again. Next, call each of your lenders to ask what they can do for you and then shop around further on the Web. (Type "student loan consolidation" into any browser and you'll get hundreds of hits.)

Remember, you're not shopping based on interest rate. The rate you'll receive—the weighted average of all loans you consolidate rounded up to the nearest one-eighth percentage point—will be the same at all lenders. (They have the ability to offer you a lower rate, but they generally don't.) Instead, you're looking for

- Future rate discounts for good behavior. Sallie Mae, for example, offers borrowers who have at least $10,000 in debt a rate discount of 1 percent when they make their first 48 monthly payments on time.
- A discount (generally one-quarter of 1 percent) for having monthly payments directly debited from your account.

Don't delay, particularly if you're in your grace period (or if the calendar is headed toward July 1, when rates change each year). If you consolidate while you're still in the six-month grace period after school ends but before repayment begins, you get an extra 0.6-point break on the interest rate. The trade-off is that you have to start repayment on the consolidated loan immediately. So if you have yet to land a job, you may want to drag out the transaction until you near the end of the grace period.

Carefully consider the term you agree to. Most student loans are scheduled to be paid back over a 10-year time frame, but most people extend the term when they consolidate to 15, 20 or even 30 years (the term you're eligible for depends on the size of your balance). This is not necessarily a bad thing. Although it will increase the total interest you pay over the life of your loan, it will give you relief right now, when you need it most. As your financial situation improves, you can prepay on your loan and get out having paid less interest to the system.

Note that although consolidating is a great move for some borrowers, it's not the best move for all borrowers. If you have an older loan and you've qualified for discounts on your rate by making 24 or 48 on-time payments, consolidating may mean swapping back to a higher rate than you already have. Also, holders of Perkins loans should be wary. Check with your lender to see if, by consolidating, you'll lose the chance to put your loan on hold for a while (or to have the government pay back the interest) if you take certain public sector jobs or go back to school.

How much do you stand to save each month? Lenders say that consolidators lower their monthly payments by $150 on average. You can run your loans through the calculator at loanconsolidation.ed.gov (the Web site of Federal Student Aid) to get an exact number.

Found Money: $_____/month

Find the Money: Refinance Your Mortgage

We have just come through the greatest refinance boom in history, and unfortunately every expert believes that rates are headed up, not down. They may be right, but that doesn't mean that the door to refinancing is closed to you today ... or forever.

There are a lot of different scenarios for which refinancing makes sense. You should consider it to cut your monthly payment when:

- Interest rates have fallen since you took out your loan, even by just a half to three-quarters of a point.
- You missed the opportunity to refinance before. Don't kick yourself for missing the bottom of the market. If today's interest rates still make it possible for you to save enough money for you to do the deal, then by all means do it.
- Your credit score has improved by 25 points or more. The lower your score was when you got your

original mortgage, the more these improvements mean. For example, jumping from an already good score of 690 to an even better one of 715 would save you almost a half a point. But jumping the same 25 points from a rotten score of 610 to a 635 that's fair to middling saves you a full 1.1 percent.

- You've paid down enough of your mortgage to turn a jumbo loan into a conforming loan. The interest rate on jumbo loans runs about one-quarter of a percentage point higher than the rate on conforming loans. A loan for a single-family house is considered "jumbo" when you're borrowing more than $333,700.

  (*Note:* This is the 2004 number. This number tends to rise a bit every year or so.)

- You're going to lose your house. Sometimes, even if you can't cut your interest rate, your situation is dire enough that you need to think about stretching out the term of your loan. The farther along you are into your mortgage, the more you'll be able to lower your payments. Say you have a $200,000 mortgage that you took out five years earlier when rates were about 7 percent. You've managed to make your monthly payments of $1,330.60 for the last half-decade, but lately it's become difficult and you've been falling behind. The good news is that you've made a dent in your loan, but you still owe $188,263. You can borrow at the same 7 percent rate (you can't get the bottom of the rate chart because you've been falling behind) for a longer term—say, thirty years—which reduces your monthly payment to $1,252.51. Your savings each month: $78.09—nearly $1,000 a year.

So, how do you proceed? Call your current lender and ask about a "streamlined refi." That's an abbreviated form of a refi with less paperwork, fewer administrative hassles and substantially lower costs. If you can't get your lender to play ball, then shop around.

There is no one source for the best rates on a mortgage these days. Check local lenders, on-line lenders and mortgage brokers to see who can give you the best rate—and whether any of them can give you a rate that makes the deal worth doing. If you find a rate that works for you, *lock it in*. Rates can move as much as a half a point from week to week. If they go up, you might find your window has closed.

Found Money: $_____/month

Find the Money: Get Rid of Mortgage Insurance

Mortgage insurance (sometimes called PMI, for Private Mortgage Insurance) can be quite expensive. It's also not optional. You have to carry mortgage insurance if you put down less than 20 percent (in the form of a down payment) when you buy a house. It costs you from $16 a month to $50 a month on every $100,000 you borrow in the form of a mortgage. And the way it works for loans made after July 1998 is that your lender has to cancel your mortgage insurance once you've accrued equity in your home of 78 percent.

The wrinkle comes when the value of your home appreciates rapidly, as it's done in many parts of the country over the last few years. All of that appreciation belongs to you, not the lender, and it may boost your ownership stake above the 20 percent mark. When that happens, you should try to get rid of your mortgage insurance.

As long as you have two full years of payments behind you, your first move should be to to ask your lender to consider allowing you to drop it. The lender will require you to have your house appraised and you will have to pay for that appraisal, so you'll need to make a decision about whether it's worth spending

some money up front to save some over the next couple of years. An appraisal will run, generally, in the
$350 range. If you plan on staying in the house (and
not refinancing) for more months than it would take
you to pay that back, it makes sense to proceed. But
you will want to have a good indication that you're
right about the value of your home *before* you pay that
appraisal money. So check the sale prices of comparable homes in your neighborhood, visit a Web site like
Domania.com or call in a Realtor to find out what your
house would list for.

The unfortunate thing is that your lender doesn't
have to accept your appraisal. Your lender may decline
it or may require a second opinion, and if you opt to
get one, you have to pay for that too.

Which brings me to option number two: refinance. If
you have been paying on your loan for less than two
years, if you don't like your lender (for whatever reason)
or if you get an indication from your lender that no
matter how your appraisal comes in, getting rid of your
mortgage insurance will be an uphill climb, refinancing
is the other way to unload this costly burden. When you
refinance, your house is appraised. That seals the value.
As long as you borrow less than 20 percent of the value
of your home in the form of a new mortgage (which you

will automatically do as long as you don't pull cash out), there will be no insurance premium on the new loan.

How much could you save? You'll generally pay anywhere from a quarter of a percentage point to three-quarters of a point of the money you borrow for mortgage insurance. The less you put down, the more of a risk the lender is taking and the higher that fraction will be. Mortgage insurance on adjustable-rate mortgages (ARMs) costs more than insurance on fixed-rate loans because ARMs are a riskier product for lenders (the default rate rises as the interest rate climbs). The easiest way to get an accurate assessment of how much this transaction will pad your pocket? See what you're paying now.

Found Money: $_____/month

How'd You Do?

So, how much found money were you able to come up with? Add up the numbers on the previous 21 pages and let's get a sense of how you're doing.

At $100 a month, you're one-third of the way there.
At $200 a month, you're over the halfway hump.

At $300 and change, you did it. In this one move, you did it.

Found Money: $_____/month

In any case, I'll bet you're feeling pretty good. Move onto the next chapter and I'll help you both find even more money and feel even better.

Another Option for Seniors

Find the Money: Reverse Mortgages

Reverse mortgages are loans that allow you to borrow back the equity in your principal residence. Just as you once paid the bank, the bank instead pays you—and at the same time allows you to stay in your home.

If you think that sounds pretty appealing, you're not the only one. Homeowners have started taking out record numbers of these loans. Why? In part it's due to marketing. Campaigns to make seniors more aware of the availability of these loans have sparked interest. But seniors strapped by falling retirement account balances and increases in the cost of medical care are also looking for new sources of cash to maintain their standards of living. Low mortgage rates haven't hurt either.

They make it possible to draw more dollars out of your house than you've been able to get in prior years.

So, how do you know if this relatively new type of loan is right for you—or your parents? First, a little background. You have to be 62 or over to qualify for a reverse mortgage. The amount you can borrow depends on your age, the value of your home and interest rates. There is no credit or income requirement. There are no monthly payments to make. And the loan doesn't have to be paid back until you sell the home, die or move out for a period of a year or more.

If you take a reverse mortgage, you can get your payout in several ways: as a line of credit, a monthly payment, a lump sum or some combination of all three. The line of credit is the most popular, but each has its benefits. A monthly payment is a guarantee of income for as long as you live in the house. A lump sum can be used to purchase an annuity that could provide you with lifetime income. If you choose the line of credit, you don't have to pay interest on money that you haven't withdrawn; in fact, your line of credit will *earn* interest while it's waiting to be used. (To get a sense of the sort of money you could reasonably expect to get from a reverse mortgage, check the "calculator" at aarp.org/revmort/.)

That doesn't mean you won't have any expenses to pay. If you have a mortgage remaining on the house, part of your payout will go to pay off *that* loan before you can draw the first dime. And you'll still be responsible for taxes, homeowners insurance and the general upkeep of the home. In fact, since the bank will actually own your house, you may be forced to pay the money back if you slide on these things. When you die or vacate the house, the amount you (or your heirs) will have to repay is the value of what you borrowed plus interest, but it can never exceed the total value (i.e., the sale price) of the home. If there's anything left after the sale of the home and the payment to the lender, you or your heirs get to keep it.

How much does it cost to get a reverse mortgage? Costs are very similar to those associated with a traditional mortgage. There are appraisal fees, origination fees, legal fees, the cost of a credit check, document prep fees, etc. Generally, though, most of these costs can be rolled into your loan, which means you pay them by getting a little less from the lender each month.

The good news is that although the costs are similar to those for a regular mortgage, the shopping process is much simpler. For 95 percent of people interested in a reverse mortgage, the best deal going is a federally insured Home Equity Conversion Mortgage (HECM), from the Federal Housing Authority or FHA. (For a list of lenders that offer HECM loans, go to the Web site of the Department of Housing and Urban Development at HUD.gov.) Unlike traditional mortgages, interest rates on HECM loans are preset; they don't vary from lender to lender.

The remaining question: Is a reverse mortgage right for

you? Before you can apply for a reverse mortgage, you have to go through counseling from HUD. These counselors will explain how the loans work. They'll use software to run what-if scenarios so that you can see how much money you'll receive. They'll explain what other options there may be. After you go through counseling, you can make a formal application. In general, however, reverse mortgages are best for:

- People who have considered moving and decided it's not right for them. It's important before you opt for a reverse mortgage to consider alternatives. For example, if you sold your house today, could you afford to buy another, smaller, one and bank some money to live on? By taking the time to shop for condos and other places to live in your area, you may actually find something you like better.
- People who have discussed this with their families. Are you keeping your house because you really want it—or because you think your children do? If it's the latter, have you taken the time to confirm that with your kids? You might be surprised to learn they feel otherwise.
- People who've exhausted their other options for support. Borrowing money (and that's what you're doing with a reverse mortgage) shouldn't be considered until you determine that there's no other source—supplemental social security, additional Medicare or Medicaid benefits—for

funds. Call the Department of Social Services in your area and speak to a counselor.

- People who have an immediate need for the money. If you don't need the income from a reverse mortgage today— even if you believe this is the solution for you—bide your time. As you age, the amount of money you'll qualify to draw will increase, making it an even more attractive option.

- People who plan to stay in their homes for at least five years. Even if you end up living in your home well past your life expectancy, the bank is obligated to keep paying you (if you chose a monthly sum) or to allow you to live there essentially rent-free. Also, if the value of your home hits a roadblock, the bank may end up paying you more than it's actually worth. But, if you die, sell or move within a few years of taking out a reverse mortgage, then it could be costly to you or your heirs—just as a traditional home loan would be, with its origination and closing costs and the cost of flipping the property in short order.

Found Money: $_____ __

STEP 6

Find the Money:
Consolidating Your Debts

ONSOLIDATING YOUR debts isn't the same thing as refinancing your debts. Consolidating—in technical terms—means taking debt from more than one source and rolling it up into one, hopefully lower, interest rate. In practical terms, however, consolidating is often just an excuse to charge those paid-off credit cards right back up again, and that can be very, very dangerous. Most people consolidate by taking out a home equity loan or line of credit. They use the proceeds from that transaction to pay off their credit card debt. Others refinance their mortgages and simultaneously pull out some cash and use *that* money to pay down their credit card bills. Either way, you've taken an unsecured debt (a debt with no assets behind it) and turned it into a secured debt. You've put your home on the line to pay off your credit card bills.

What you got for taking this risk was the ability to pay off what was probably very high–rate credit card debt at a rate that's not only much, much lower, but tax deductible. Let's say you're carrying $20,000 of credit card debt at 18 percent. If you put aside $10 a day, it'll take you 24 years to pay that off. At 4 percent, you'll be able to do it in one–third the time, *and* you get to deduct the interest you pay on your tax return. In other words, there are considerable advantages to consolidating. That's why so many people are doing it. According to the Consumer Bankers Association, home equity loans and lines of credit now account for more than half of all consumer credit.

The good news is that many people, according to new research from the Federal Reserve of New York, have been smart about how they have used those funds. Between 2001 and 2003, according to the study, homeowners refinanced $5 trillion worth of mortgage debt. About one–quarter of that money went out the door in the form of cash. What did we do with all that money? We spent some of it, of course, keeping our economy afloat, but 35 percent of the money went into home improvements (a smart use since it adds to the value of the underlying asset) and 26 percent went to pay down high-rate credit card debt. We invested 21 percent in a combination of stock and other financial and real estate investments (which is okay if the return on those investments exceeds the rate of interest we're paying on the loan). And we spent 16 percent on cars, vacations and education (all but the latter are questionable uses since we'll be paying for the purchases long after they were used up).

We clearly have the right intentions, but here's the thing: one-third of people who use cash-out refis and home equity loans to pay off their credit card bills then proceed to charge their credit cards right back up. Then they're not just right back where they started from; they're in far worse shape, because now they have to pay back *both* loans.

So, you have to be sure of your willpower before you proceed with a consolidation loan. Do you have the ability to pay off those credit cards and then not use them again? Do you have the fortitude? Will you be able to tough it out, even if it means not buying the things you want—or worse, the things your kids are asking you for? If you're not sure, then don't do this deal. *Don't.* Lower your interest rates as far as you can with the methods I described in the previous chapter. Work on your credit score so that you can bring the rates down even further, but don't put yourself in the path of temptation. It's just not worth it.

If you decide to proceed, you need to do everything possible to help yourself from falling off the wagon. Even if you're completely confident in your ability to steer clear of your plastic, you need to set up a system of roadblocks that will get in your way before you overspend and overcharge. I'm dead serious about this. I don't care if you believe you've got the willpower of a Miss America constestant cutting carbs. Remember: one-third of people who pay off their credit card bills with consolidation have big credit card bills again in short order. You don't think they all *planned* to climb back in the hole, do you?

So, what sort of safeguards are in order?

- Get rid of all but one or two low-rate credit cards. As I noted earlier in the book, this will not be good for your credit score, part of which is based on the ratio of the credit you're using to your available credit lines. Closing accounts will cause that ratio to drop. But unless you're planning to apply for a mortgage or car loan in the next year, it's not a big deal. You're better off not having a walletful of temptation.

- Turn down credit line increases on those cards—in fact, think about reducing the ones you have. You can only get into as much trouble as your credit lines will allow. Turning down a credit line increase (or asking for a reduction) is as easy as calling the toll–free number on the back of your card.

- Take those credit cards out of your wallet and carry a debit card instead. If you're using a debit card, you can't spend money you don't have. Even frequent–flier–mile junkies have debit cards to choose from these days. No, you don't get quite as many miles, but it doesn't matter. They're not worth as much as they used to be anyway.

- Write checks and pay cash. For many people, it's tougher psychologically to part with their cash or write a check than it is to slide a piece of plastic through a little electronic slot. It feels more real, and it is. Why? Because once the money's gone, it's really gone.

- Create small stashes for big goals. Let's say you decide you really want to go on vacation at the end of
  the year with your family. You're on track putting
  aside your $10 a day, and you don't want to let a
  short-term splurge get in the way of your long-
  term success. And you certainly don't want to
  charge it. How do you handle it? Create another
  savings pool. If you know that vacation is going to
  run $1,500 and you're five months out, then another
  $10 a day will get you to your goal. By rustling up
  the money beforehand, you'll be able to enjoy
  yourself and not feel guilty afterward.

- Tell your friends, family and anyone else you're
  likely to (window) shop with what you're up to. If
  you clue your inner circle into the fact that you're
  trying not to charge (indeed, that you're trying not
  to spend), they'll help you with that quest rather
  than suggest you spend your lunch hour trying on
  boots at Bloomingdale's. If on-line shopping is your
  particular weakness, tell your roommate, office-
  mate, spouse or anyone else who's likely to see you
  succumb. In fact, you may want to dub one of them
  your debt buddy—preferably someone who's fac-
  ing the same financial challenges you are. Then you
  can talk your way through.

Which Loan Do You Want?

Once your safeguards are in place and you're ready to proceed, you need to understand the consolidation landscape in order to get the best deal. That means understanding home equity loans and home equity lines of credit as well as cash-out refinances of your mortgage, starting with the fact that they are three very different animals. Here's a look at what they are, what they're good for and where—typically—you'll find the best deals.

Home equity loans are fixed-rate loans. They're available in terms ranging from 5 years to 15 years, though 10-year terms are the most common. When you take a home equity loan, you borrow the money all at once and start repaying it immediately.

- *They're best for* projects where you need the money in one big chunk—like redoing your kitchen.
- *Good deals* generally come from your bank (your local bank, in fact) or credit union. Closing costs vary widely, from about $300 to about $500, so shop around.

Home equity lines of credit (HELOC) are variable-rate loans with interest rates that are usually tied to the prime rate (with a lifetime interest rate cap of around 18 percent). They, too, typically have terms of 10 years. Unlike home equity loans, however, having a *line* of credit means you don't have to borrow all the money at once. You receive the equivalent of a checkbook and withdraw (and of course pay back) funds as you need them.

- *They're best for* money you need to use over time. You only pay interest on the money you've withdrawn, which makes it a good use for costs you'll incur over several years, such as a home renovation you're approaching room by room, or college tuition. After all, why would you want to pay interest on the whole chunk of money when you're not using it all?

- *Good deals* are found by shopping around. Compare annual fees (generally around $50), and beware of teaser rates. They're compelling, but you need to ask, "Then what happens?" Six months of very low interest means very little on a loan you're paying back over a decade.

A cash-out refinance is when you go back to the mortgage well and draw out additional equity, either that you've paid into the home or that has become yours

through appreciation. For example, let's say you originally took out a $150,000 mortgage to buy a $200,000
home. Interest rates are lower than they were previously and you'd like to take advantage of that. But you
also need $20,000 to pay back some high-rate credit
card debt. You can refinance the loan for $170,000, so
that you get the $150,000 you owe and the additional
$20,000 at a lower interest rate. You're not taking out a
second mortgage, as you are with HELOCs and home
equity loans; you're replacing your first mortgage. This
has advantages and disadvantages. The advantages are
that as long as you aren't drawing out all (or more than)
the equity in your home, the interest rate will generally
be lower than on the other options, and that a greater
amount of mortgage interest is tax deductible The disadvantages are that you'll face additional costs—a new
appraisal and closing costs—just like any other refi.

- *They're best for* borrowers who've seen a drop in interest rates since they last took out a mortgage (or
  refinanced). It doesn't make sense to pay a higher
  interest rate on all the money you owe on your
  house. If rates have gone up and you still need to
  draw funds from your house, you're better off with
  a home equity loan or a HELOC, which will allow

you to pay the higher interest rate on just the incremental chunk. One thing to watch out for: mortgage insurance. If you've moved beyond owing PMI (either by paying down more than 20 percent of your home, or because of appreciation), another round of borrowing could put you right back in PMI territory. That amount alone may be more than the difference in interest rates between a HELOC/ home equity loan and a refi. In that case, you're better off with the latter. And, particularly if you've been in your home more than five years, be wary of extending the term of your loan. See if you can use the lower rates to shorten your term to 15, 20, even 25 years. (Lenders are being increasingly flexible.) You don't want to be paying off your mortgage as you head into your retirement years.

- *Good deals* are found by shopping around as you did when you originally got your mortgage. Check on-line sources, mortgage brokers and your local bank or credit union before locking in your deal.

Tales of Life and Debt: A Step in the Right Direction— Consolidating Your Debts

Laurie, a subscriber to my Web site, JeanChatzky.com, sent me this e-mail:

I started with substantial savings of $16,000. Now I'm down to $800 with a great deal of credit card debt. I make a good salary, but I just can't seem to figure how to start paying off my credit cards. One is at about $30,000 and I have others that are much smaller. I am basically paralyzed. . . . Can you please help me? I am extremely intelligent and embarrassed that I have so little financial sense.

A few days later, I gave Laurie a call. I learned that she is a paralegal, living on Sheppard Air Force Base in Texas. The $16,000 she was talking about came from her employer, who gave her a large bonus when he won a large case. She bought some furniture with about a quarter of the money, then put the rest in savings with the intent of paying down her debts.

But she got sidetracked. Actually, she got sick. Her doctor found a tumor that he suspected was uterine cancer. In the end—thankfully—it was benign, but the combination of increased medical expenses and time spent not working did a number on her savings. After she had her surgery in February 2003, she was left with a huge credit card bill and only $2,000 in the bank. Not surprisingly, her financial situation put a damper on the happiness she was feeling over her health.

In looking the numbers over together, though, we found that her situation wasn't as bad as she feared. First of all, Laurie and her husband—who's in the military—don't have a mortgage. That means all of their earnings can go to paying their bills and other living expenses. She spends more than she has to on eating out and clothing—both areas in which she's willing to cut back. They are currently paying $9,000 a year in college tuition for their son. But since he's halfway through his junior year, they can also see an end in sight. The $6,000 a year they're paying for car insurance—not for their car, for their insurance!—is exhorbitant, but Laurie admits she hasn't shopped around for a better deal. And the interest rates on their credit cards are higher than they have to be. Again, Laurie hadn't even attempted to bring them down.

That was the assignment I gave her. Call your credit card companies and ask—just ask—for a reduction in your interest rates. If they tell you no, then ask for a supervisor. It wasn't even 24 hours later that she sent me the following e-mail:

I first called the credit card company with the largest debt. There is, of course, no option on the automatic menu for anyone who actually just wants to talk to a customer rep-

resentative. . . . In this case, I chose the option of "Making a Change to My Account." When I actually was connected to a real person, I explained that I wanted to discuss decreasing my interest rate. At that point, I was transferred to an "account manager." The account manager was exceptionally helpful and respectful when I explained my situation (serious health crisis with resulting increase in debt). She checked (about 3 minutes) and came back on the line to tell me she could give me a 10.99 percent rate. She said I could check back in 5–6 months. At that point, I clarified with her that the 5–6 months was not a limit on the period of 10.99 percent interest—but that the interest rate would be that way indefinitely unless I made a late payment or went over my credit limit, at which time it could go up to 24.99 percent. According to the account rep (whose name I wrote down), the 5–6 months means that I can check back then and see about the possibility of getting a further reduction in the interest rate. I was told this rate would go into effect on February 17. This is definitely an improvement from the 14.99 percent rate I had before.

The second card company was a little easier in that there is actually (if you listen long enough) an option in the first menu to speak to a customer representative. I explained to the woman with whom I was connected that I had had a severe health crisis which resulted in increased debt—I really wanted to pay off the balance but the interest rate was killing me. I also mentioned having to transfer to another card with lower interest rate. In this instance, she said that she could help me herself (no need to transfer to an "account manager"). She, too, was friendly. However, after putting me on hold for about 2 minutes, she came back and said she could not help me. She said the 12.99 percent interest rate I have is the lowest available for that particular type of card. In hindsight, I might have asked to speak to her supervisor but I did not do so.

With the third card company, I waited until I got a real person. I again explained what I needed and was transferred to an "account specialist." Again, the representative was friendly and helpful. She put me on hold for about 4 minutes, came back and said she could get me a 12.99 percent rate. I told her that since I already had a 13.99 percent rate, that wouldn't give me much relief. She then said she could offer me a 10.99 percent rate. I agreed and confirmed that the rate would stay the same unless I was late or exceeded my credit limit. I asked if it could ever go up at any time and she said it was an adjustable rate; it could go up but she would not anticipate it since interest rates were so low and predicted to stay that way. Again, I got the rep's name in case there was a problem. I was told this rate would go into effect immediately.

My husband and I both realize that my debts are the ones we need to work on since his are small in comparison to mine and we can surely work on his after we've learned how to manage mine. We both want desperately to get our debt under control so we can purchase a house when he retires from the military in 4–5 years.

As I told Laurie, she can take comfort in knowing that she's taken a step in the right direction.

STEP 7

Find the Money: Spending Less

WHY DO WE spend money? Sometimes it's be-cause we need something. We need to fix the leak in the roof. We need a car (or other form of trans-portation) to get us back and forth to work. We need day care for our children so we can go to those jobs. We need food to put on the table and appropriate clothing to put on our bodies. We need a telephone to keep in touch with our offices, our spouses, to call the author-ities in an emergency. We need decent medical care.

But mostly we spend because we want things. We want to go out to dinner because we've just had a long day or week. We want a cell phone in addition to our landline because we want to be reachable anytime, anywhere. We want to look better and feel better than we feel right now—and we think that spending money on new shoes, a new car or new makeup or a bag will help us do just that. When you stop and think about it, you have to admit that's where a great deal of your money goes.

We need certain things—and we want others. That's the top explanation for where every bit of your money goes. But, if you're one of those people who feels they shop a little too much (and come on, who doesn't feel like that occasionally?), there's probably a more deep-rooted reason for your behavior.

Sue Eccles and Helen Woodruff-Burton, two British researchers, took an academic look in 2000 at why we go shopping. They believe that when we shop for anything other than the true basics, it's because we're missing something else in our lives. The catch phrase for this behavior is called "retail therapy," but in academic circles it's called "compensatory consumption." And they've put their fingers on seven reasons why we engage in it:

- We're bored ... with our lives, our looks, our cars and appliances. When we shop out of boredom, we're looking for a pick-me-up.

- We're depressed and need an escape from reality. Shopping is a more socially acceptable escape from dealing with deep unhappiness than are alcohol or drugs. New research has shown, however, that it can be just as unhealthy.

- We want to "get a life." ... We're underwhelmed with the look and shape our life has taken, so we spend to produce a better-looking, fuller-feeling one.

- We want to improve our moods. Shopping, for some people, brings a feeling of excitement, the "high" of getting a good deal. Shopping is a mission. The idea of a trip to the mall or your favorite boutique sets your toes tingling, a little like a caffeine buzz.

- We are trying to assert our independence over our parents, then our partners. ... In marriages and other relationships that aren't functioning well, one spouse may overspend to teach the other "you don't own me."

- We want to feel more attractive. ... We are convinced that if we only had that dress (that tie, those shoes), we'd look 100 times better.

- We're on autopilot. ... It's been so long since we *didn't* drop that $5 a day on coffee and a bagel that we do it without thinking about it—even when we're not hungry, even when we don't really want it. We get into patterns with our shopping just as we do with many other things in our lives. Sometimes, those patterns are tough to break.

I share these reasons with you because I believe that knowing why you're doing something—knowing why you're engaging in a particular behavior—can help you to get a grip on it. Until you understand why you've got 10 pairs of shoes in your closet that you really don't need, for example, or stacks of CDs that you have yet to listen to, it's tougher to stop yourself from purchasing the eleventh pair or another disc.

Women, research shows, are more likely to spend on nonnecessities (and therefore overspend) than men. That's probably because we're the ones who do most of the spending overall. Since the nineteenth century, women have done about 80 percent of our country's shopping. That ratio remains fairly consistent, even today. Originally, we gravitated to shops because they—unlike pubs and bars—were one of the few places a woman could go alone without worrying about her safety or her reputation. Department stores caught onto these shopping patterns and, as they developed, outfitted themselves to attract women who had money to spend. Today, though, it's not just in the stores that women are outspending men. During the 2003 holiday season, women outspent men on-line—driving big gains in categories like clothing and accessories. Unfortunately, women are also less likely to haggle. According to research for the book *Women Don't Ask: Negotiation and the Gender Divide* by Linda Babcock and Sara Lascherer (Princeton University Press, 2003), female car buyers will pay as much as $1,353 (yikes!) to *avoid* negotiating the price of a car.

What we're going to do in this step is go through the lists of all the different things you spend money on each month. For each item, you need to ask yourself: Is this necessary? If it's not, then I want you to rank it—high priority, medium priority, low priority. (I'm going to share with you how I'd rank the items as well, and although it's perfectly fine for your rankings to be different from mine—you and I probably do have different needs—it's not okay for everything you spend money on to be a high priority. Your expenditures should split fairly equally among the three categories. Be sure you fill in the savings you calculate on the blank after "Found Money" for each item.) Then, we'll see if there's a way to trim your costs and by how much. At the end of the exercise, you'll see how much money you were able to free up.

(*Note*: Don't just skip over the line for "other." I have put into this work sheet just about everything I could think of, but as I said, you and I have different lives. This exercise only works if you're really honest about where your money is going today.)

Fixed Expenses

• *Rent/Mortgage:* High priority. Consider refinancing. See step 6.

Found money: $_____

• *Common charges (condo fees, etc.):* High priority. Non-negotiable.
• *Car payment 1:* High priority. Consider refinancing. See step 6.

Found money: $_____

• *Car payment 2:* Medium priority. A second car, no doubt, really makes your life easier, but do you need it? Could one of you drive the other to work or drop the other off at a bus or train station? Could you carpool with a coworker? I know that this means trading convenience for savings, but that's what this entire exercise is about. If you need the car, consider refinancing as a way to save money on your loan. If you're driving a rel-atively new or relatively expensive car, consider selling it, paying off your loan and buying a cheaper, older model. That will save you money each month. For how-to information, see step 6.

Found money: $_____

• *Car payment 3:* Low priority. A third car? I've heard a number of explanations for why this is necessary. You need a car for the sitter to drive or for your high schooler to get back and forth to his or her activities. I'm dubious. But if your high schooler truly needs this car, then he or she should be helping to pay for it by earning money to foot the bill for insurance, gas, even a portion of the payment if possible. Still, maybe there's another way. Maybe your spouse could drop you off at work and your teen could pick you up. Again, if you really do need it, refinance the loan if you haven't already. But you're going to need to trim elsewhere.

Found money: $_____

• *Train ticket, parking and other commuting expenses:* High priority. Have you run the numbers to see which is the most economical way to commute? By bus? By train?

By car? Have you shopped around for the cheapest parking solution? Have you looked into carpooling so that you don't have to pay for parking everyday? Call your benefits department to see if your company has a transportation savings account, which works like a flexible spending account. It allows you to pay for transportation expenses, including parking, with pre-tax dollars, which will save you one-quarter to one-third of the cost.

Found money: $_____

• *Child support:* High priority. Your child deserves your support. However, if you are in a situation in which you cannot pay, notify your child support agency immediately. If you've become ill or disabled and can't work, you can ask the court to review your support order to restructure or reduce your payments. No found money here.

• *Alimony:* High priority. If you've agreed to pay alimony, then of course you should pay it. However, you should also know that the courts believe failing to pay child support is generally *much worse* than failing to pay alimony. No found money here either.

• *Back taxes:* High priority. Call the IRS and see if you can work out a payment schedule that makes sense for you. They are notoriously flexible if they know that they'll eventually get their money. The important thing to stress is that you want to pay but that you're having trouble making ends meet right now.

• *Student loan payment:* High priority. Consider consolidating. See step 6.

Found money: $_____

• *Credit card payments:* High priority. As we've established, only *after* you dig out of credit card debt will you be able to make true progress with the rest of your financial goals. That makes this a high–priority line item. Work to lower your interest rates to make payoff faster, less expensive. See step 6.

Found money: $_____

• *Utilities:* High priority. There aren't a lot of places in the country—except the state of Texas—where switching to an alternate energy provider can save you money. (Go to www.energyguide.com to see if you have options in your area.) What you can do is buy better appliances (when yours die, of course; buying new ones before you need them is a spending exercise, not a saving one) and then take care of them. A home outfitted with appliances that have the Energy Star logo will cost

30 percent less a year to run than one without. To help your heater or furnace work more efficiently, check the air filters once a month and clean (washable ones are available) or replace them if they're dirty (that can save $50 in heating a year). Buying a thermostat that adjusts automatically at night can knock another 10 percent off your utility bills. And caulk and seal or put weather stripping around drafty windows and doors. Check with your local utility company to see if they offer any other ways to earn discounts or credits on your bills.

Found money: $_____

• *Health club:* Low priority. This is one of those things that you pay for every month that you may not even use. If you don't go more than once a week, you absolutely need to cancel your membership. Even if you do go, consider canceling your membership or at least putting it on hold until you dig out. Could you pay a less expensive rate to just take a class occasionally? Could you run or walk (or engage in some other free pursuit) outside? If you feel you really need a gym (and I understand that for some people, it's a matter of sanity), check with your company benefits department. Many offer health club discounts. Also look to see if your health insurer offers any sort of reimbursement. Then shop around to see if you can find a better deal. Once you've secured one (it won't be difficult), go back to the gym you belong to and see if you can use your new rate to bargain for a discount. Explain you may have to leave unless they can give you a break on the monthly dues. If that doesn't work, you'll have to switch.

Found money: $_____

• *Internet:* Medium priority. If you have e-mail access at work, consider canceling your Internet service at home (chances are you're using it to shop unnecessarily anyway). If you use the Internet to work at home, then you probably do need it. Try to get your employer to foot your bills. If you work for yourself, shop around for a better deal. Many people still maintain a separate second phone line in their homes for dial-up Internet access. If you're one of them, you can probably save a good deal by getting rid of that second line and switching to broadband, where introductory deals abound.

Found money: $_____

• *Cable:* Low priority. If you can do without it and still get basic TV, cancel. If not, go to basic.

(*Note:* I know there are some people who can go without TV altogether. I am most definitely not one of them . . . so I won't be suggesting you go cold turkey either.)

Found money: $_____

• *Phone service (landline and cellular)*: The best way to save money on your phone bills is to bundle all the services you need on one phone and go bare-bones on the other. Many people have decided they can go so bare that they can drop their landlines entirely, but I wouldn't advise it if there are children in the house. You don't want to have to call 911 and find your battery has died. Dropping your wireless service entirely, on the other hand, is something you may want to think about (particularly if you're feeling very stretched). But if you're reluctant, consider this suggestion: See how much money you can save on both services by cutting back. If you can't save enough, you can drop wireless, long-distance first. If you're paying more than four cents per minute for long-distance calls (and a few cents more for in-state ones), you're paying too much. Chances are, if you're a customer of one of the country's name-brand phone companies, you're paying too much, too. Go to the calculator at MyRatePlan.com and tell the computer where you live, how much you talk and where you call. It'll spit out a better plan. Then do the same for wireless. If you've decided your wireless phone will be your primary phone (and that you'll use the landline for emergencies and basic local service), look for a wireless plan that gives you unlimited nights and weekends. If you've decided your landline is your primary, you can get a basic wireless plan for about $20 a month. Again, the MyRatePlan.com calculator can help. Then stick to your plan. If you decide your wireless phone will be your primary, don't make long-distance calls on your landline. If you decide your landline will be your primary, don't use your wireless to order pizza.

Found money: $_____

• *Wireless device (PDA):* Low priority. You are never going to convince me that you need this. Why? Because you lived without it for so many years. If you use it for work, try convincing your employer to pay for it. If you're unsuccessful, cancel your service as soon as your contract is up.

(*Note:* If the penalty for canceling before your contract has expired is small compared to what you would pay for the remainder of your service, cancel today.)

Found money: $_____

• *Child care/baby-sitter:* Set up a dependent care spending account through your employer (the vast majority of companies offer this option), which allows you to pay for day care using pretax dollars. That move alone can save you 30 percent on your tab. And if one of you is out of work, it makes no sense to employ a baby-sitter for children of school age. You can look for work that needs you from 8 until the kids get out at 3. Then you can work for the family.

Found money: $_____

• *Health insurance:* Call your benefits department and see if there is a less-expensive plan you could switch to within your company. If you and your spouse are both working for employers that offer coverage, it probably will make sense for each of you to take coverage from your own company (unless one employer covers families for free) rather than doubling up. If you are paying for your own insurance, go to eHealthInsurance.com, an insurance Web site, to see if it's possible to switch to a less-expensive plan.

Found money: $_____

• *Homeowners and auto insurance:* If it's been a while since you shopped around for these coverages, you're probably paying more than you have to. Call an independent insurance agent (one who can quote you policies from a variety of carriers) and shop on the Internet as well. Buying both of these policies from a single carrier can net you a significant discount. There are also discounts if you've stopped smoking, improved security in your home, been with a particular insurer for more than three years, or hit your fifty-fifth birthday (seniors generally stay home more, spend more time maintaining their homes and drive less, and insurers reward them for this). But you'll get the biggest savings by raising your deductibles. Your deductible is the amount of money you'll have to pay out-of-pocket *before* your insurance coverage kicks in. Typically, most deductibles start at $250. If you raise yours to $500, you'll save up to 12 percent. Go even higher—to $1,000—and you can save up to 24 percent. You can go higher still and save 30 percent or more, but be sure that you don't go too high for your wallet.

Found money: $_____

• *Life insurance:* High priority. If you're single and have no dependents (either kids or older parents you support), you don't need life insurance. Unless it's coverage your company provides for free, get rid of it. If you have dependents, then life insurance becomes a high–priority item, but you have to buy smart and that means that if you're in cost–cutting mode, you shouldn't be buying any form of permanent insurance (whole life, universal life, annuities). You should be buying term life insurance. Term life insurance is a death benefit with nothing else attached. It covers you only while you pay for it (generally for a term of 10 to 30 years) and for that reason it's much, much cheaper than permanent insurance. The other way to find cheaper rates is to buy group insurance, generally through your employer. You may have to pay for it, but it can be less expensive than comparable plans you'll find shopping alone. What if you've already started paying for a cash–value/permanent policy and you're having trouble making the payments? Call your insurer. You may have the ability to convert the policy to a term life policy based on the cash you've already accumulated. You can also cash out. You'll no longer be covered by the insurance, but you can use the money to pay down your existing debts and then replace it with cheaper term life.

(*Note:* Don't cancel your existing insurance policy until you secure a new one. You will have to undergo a physical exam for a new policy. If your health has changed [and not for the better], you may find the cost of a new policy prohibitive; worse, you may find that you can't qualify at all.)

Found money: $_____

• *Regular prescriptions:* High priority. Yes, these are non-negotiable items. Yes, you can also save money. How? By making sure you buy generic drugs rather than name brands where available. If you're on Medicare, obtaining one of the new drug discount cards can save you 10 to 17 percent annually—more if you're a low-income individual: then you get a $600 credit toward your prescription drugs. Consider ordering from an on-line pharmacy as well, where the number of pills in a single prescription can be substantially cheaper.

Found money: $_____

• *Payments for other purchases like furniture, appliances:* Medium priority. Although you of course want to make these payments, the fact is you can probably let them slide for a while without worrying about repossession. In order to repossess your property, the lawyers at the National Consumer Law Center point out, the lender has to get permission to come in the house, and you're unlikely to give them that. It also costs merchants so much to go through the exercise of getting back your property that many will decide it's not worth it. If you're having trouble making these payments, call your local credit union (if you don't belong to one, go to cuna.org to find one that will have you as a member) and see if you can refinance the debt through them using an unsecured personal loan. You'll pay a much lower interest rate and get rid of the other garbage—like credit insurance—that was probably packaged with the loan. Even if you face prepayment penalties (you probably will), you can probably save money. If prepayment penalties are so onerous that you don't want to switch lenders, call your current lender and ask for a reduction in the interest rate and cancel any insurance that goes with the loan.

Found money: $_____

- *Housekeeper:* Low priority. This is someone you could do without for a while.

Found money: $_____

- *Lawn care:* Low priority. Again, this becomes a do–it–yourself item.

Found money: $_____

• *Private school:* Medium priority. Most private schools (and private nursery schools) have a person on staff to deal with the issue of financial aid (you're not the only one in this boat!). Make an appointment to talk with that person, in person, to see if you can obtain financial assistance. Particularly if your child has been thriving at the school, many administrators will do everything they can to help you get through these hard times. Check out other resources for scholarships and aid as well: some employers offer scholarship programs, ask your clergy, do an Internet search and, if your child is in this school because of a special learning (or other) need, talk to your state education department about whether assistance is available. If all of these avenues fail, you will have to consider moving your child to public school.

Found money: $_____

• *Tutoring:* Medium priority. Talk to your school principal. Explain that you're having financial difficulties but that you'd like to maintain the tutoring for your child. He or she may have suggestions for free or low-cost tutoring in your area. If you're receiving tutoring through a large-scale program, talk to the director about a reduction in price until you get on your financial feet.

Found money: $_____

• *After-school programs/sports for your kids:* Medium priority. First, let's differentiate between after-school programs that allow you to finish the work day and those that don't. The first are necessities (though you should look into whether financial assistance is available or if there's a lower-cost option for which—if your children are age 13 or younger—tax breaks may be available). The latter are extras. I know, I have two children. I know that although you're willing to cut back for yourself, cutting back for your children can be heartbreaking. But this is an area in which you absolutely need to look at trying to save some money. Perhaps you could switch from a basketball program at a private facility to a cheaper one with your town's recreation department. Maybe you can drop two of four music lessons per month. Again, always ask if aid is available. If there are activities your kids constantly fight you about attending, now's the time to drop them. If the children in question are teenagers, now is a good time to talk to them about contributing to the cost of their activities by baby-sitting or getting a part-time job.

Found money: $_____

• *Church, synagogue or other religious center expenses:* Low priority. Your house of worship is one area that will almost definitely cut you a break. Schedule an appointment with a clerical leader, explain your financial situation and that you'll start paying again as soon as you're able.

Found money: $_____

• *Summer camp:* Medium priority. Again, if the only way you're able to work during the summer is by finding a camp program for your kids, camp becomes a necessity. Financial assistance and tax breaks are often available. Shop around for a good program at a good price and then apply for it (and note: any expense you incur for a child under age 13 that allows you to go to work may be deducted as part of the dependent care credit worth approximately $2,000 to your bottom line each year).

Found money: $_____

• *Other*: As you went through and tracked your monthly fixed expenses, you probably came up with several that are not listed here. Use the strategies we've discussed to try to trim your costs in those areas.

Found money: $_____

Total found money from fixed expenses:

$_____

Now it's time to attack your variable expenses. Except for groceries and gasoline, these are not going to be high-priority items—certainly not as high as paying your rent or your mortgage. That means your first step should be to see if you can free up enough money to repay your debts by shopping around. There's more flexibility there than you may think. The Consumer Literacy Consortium recently engaged a group of students at Virginia Tech University for an exercise in comparison shopping. They had the students make three phone calls each to see if they could get a better deal on plane tickets, car rentals and color TVs. They did incredibly well. After three phone calls the savings on car rentals averaged 10 percent, on televisions 20 percent and on plane tickets 50 percent. It also means you have to be willing to give up certain

items—certainly not every item on the list, and certainly not forever.

But a big part of this exercise is focusing on what
things in your life are most important to you. It involves
setting priorities and making conscious choices. Those
are the only ones you should be spending money on in
this debt–repayment stage. If you're having trouble
discriminating, ask yourself the question this way:
Which *things* are more important than your future?

To get a sense of how much money you're "finding"
in each category, figure out how much you have been
spending, on average, each month. Then figure out
how much you think you could spend on a budget.

Variable Expenses

• *Groceries*: High priority. Of course you need to eat.
But, in our time–starved world, it's very easy to fall
into the trap of shopping meal by meal. That can be
almost as expensive as eating in a restaurant. Likewise,
making lunches for your kids to take to school (and for
you to take to work) will always be less expensive than
buying them. The solution is to do what your mother
(or maybe grandmother) told you to do. Plan out a
week's worth of meals. Include a day or so of leftovers

in your schedule. Then make a list and shop for just what you need. You'll spend less on convenience foods if you try to shop only the outside aisles of the supermarket. That'll net you produce, dairy, meat and fish. If you venture inside, make sure you're going for a particular item or another. Then pay close attention to what gets eaten (and what gets wasted) in your house. Clipping coupons for items you use (not for items you want to try) can save money as well, particularly if you use them at stores that offer double or triple the value. And be sure to join the loyalty program of every supermarket in town. That way, no matter which market you decide to patronize that week, you'll get the best prices. You may, with this new meal–planning strategy, actually spend a little more in this category the first couple of weeks as you're loading up on spices and other ingredients. Don't worry, you'll recoup the money because you won't be eating out as much.

Found money: $_____

• *Restaurant meals*: Low priority. How many nights a month do you eat in a restaurant? Cut that number in half with the understanding that if that doesn't move you close enough to your goal, you may have to cut further. Also, be sure that when you do dine out, you don't do it in a way that sabotages your money-saving goals.

Found money: $_____

• *Takeout*: Low priority. Takeout is a habit more than anything else. You're not getting the experience of sitting in a nice restaurant and being served; you're opening a brown paper bag and wolfing down a sandwich at your desk. Think carefully about which of these expenses can go. Can you stomach the coffee from the office pot? That's 75 cents a cup if you've been buying from the cart on the corner, $3 a cup if you've been drinking a latte. Can you handle bringing your lunch from home rather than buying it from the local sandwich shop? You could free up your $10 a day right there. And how much money are you actually dropping into those soda and candy machines in the lounge? You know, they're not very good for your waistline either.

Found money: $_____

• *Gasoline*: High priority. If your car doesn't call for premium gasoline, use regular. Don't skimp on the oil changes that keep it running efficiently. By all means, carpool. You can find the cheapest per-gallon prices in your neighborhood at Web sites like gaspricewatch.com. (And by all means, the next time you're in the market for a car, consider getting one that doesn't guzzle.)

Found money: $_____

• *Other medical expenses (appointments that aren't reimbursed)*: High/medium priority. If you need to see a doctor, you need to see a doctor. This isn't the time, however, to be spending large sums of unreimbursed money on cosmetic procedures of any kind—for your eyes, your skin, your teeth. For those expenditures you do need to make, signing up for a flexible spending account at work allows you to pay for unreimbursed medical expenses with pretax dollars. The hitch is that you have to ballpark the amount you'll spend at the beginning of each year—and if you don't use that amount, you lose it. Call your benefits department to see if this is a possibility for you.

Found money: $_____

• *Clothing, shoes, accessories*: Medium/low priority. I'm not suggesting you never buy another pair of pants or shoes, but you need to think of these purchases in terms of whether they're actually needed—and how much you absolutely have to spend on them. New $20 sneakers for your child whose feet won't stop growing? Needed. New $50 name-brand sneakers for your child whose feet won't stop growing? I don't think so. A new black dress to wear to your cousin's wedding? Not if you have three others in the closet. It doesn't really matter that hemlines have moved. If you're not the bride, no one will be looking at you anyway. If you're looking to trim expenses rather than cutting them out entirely, you need to know how to shop the sales. Timing is everything when it comes to not paying full price. Generally, department stores take their first markdowns two months after merchandise has been on the shelves. In chain stores, those markdowns come even more rapidly. Generally, first markdowns run 20 to 30 percent. If the item you're after looks to be in short supply (or you're a tough size), that's the time to buy. If there's ample stock, you can take comfort in knowing that two weeks down the road, items will be reduced (from the original price) by 40 percent. By the time third markdowns roll around (another two weeks later), you'll see prices of up to 70 percent off. Interestingly, personal shoppers say you'll do better shopping at department stores than boutiques. Not only do they have more lenient return policies, they're more inclined to discount because if items don't sell, designers will give them credits for future merchandise.

Found money: $_____

• *Entertaining/entertainment*: Medium priority. If you take all the fun out of your life, this is not going to be a plan that you're going to be able to stick with for very long. That's why the goal here—as in many of the other categories—is to trim expenses, not eliminate them. So, instead of restaurant meals, invite friends in and do potluck. Or fill your friends in on the fact that you're trying to budget and they'll naturally start to suggest drinks instead of dinner and the local Italian joint instead of the chic and pricey brasserie. Challenge yourself to come up with cheaper ways of enjoying yourself: ice skate outside rather than indoors, show movies on pay-per-view ($3.95 and everyone can watch!) instead of going out to the movies or theater, or renting videos that can rack up late fees, and take day trips to the nearest beach rather than weekend overnighters. And if you spend more than you'd like for Saturday-night sitters, try piggybacking with friends: you take care of their kids one week, they take care of yours the next.

Found money: $_____

• *Travel*: Low priority. Yes, you have to have some fun, but while you're trying to cut back, this is one big-ticket expense that can be sharply curtailed. If you generally vacation both summer and winter, think about cutting out one of those trips—at least while you're getting on your feet. Particularly during high (read: crowded) season, vacationing at home can be just as fun—and much more restful. The key to not blowing the budget is shopping smart when you do venture out. If you're buying airline tickets, you're best off buying very early—or very late. On the most competitive routes, advertised sale fares disappear quickly, so you want to jump on board as soon as you see them in the morning paper (or your e-mail). Last-minute deals are more prevalent if you're willing to travel places many travelers won't go or be flexible on the days you're willing to leave and return (even if that means pulling your kids out of school a day early). When booking a hotel room, use the Internet to pinpoint where you want to stay and at what price, then call the hotel directly to ask if there's a better deal available. If you've racked up airline miles, using them for hotel stays is one way to maximize their value.

Found money: $_____

• *Gifts*: Medium priority. My mother always said it's the thought that counts. But she also taught me that you never show up (at a party or someone's house) empty-handed. The trick is to split the difference. If your kids are attending birthday party after birthday party, think about declining the invitations from the kids they really don't know or play with. Then buy great, inexpensive gifts in bulk whenever and wherever you find them. Warehouse stores can be great sources for these. I recently picked up a huge set of really cool markers for $5.95 (I got 10). Other tactics: Go in with friends or relatives to slice the cost of gifts in half. Plan a grab bag for the holidays so that you're buying only for a single person, not everybody. Decide to make a contribution to a friend's favorite charity (nobody needs to know how much or little you gave). Resist the urge to try to keep pace with what your more affluent (less indebted) friends are buying you. Someone has to break what often becomes a ridiculously lavish cycle; it might as well be you.

Found money: $_____

• *Newspapers and magazines*: Low priority. First, cancel anything you're not reading. Second, if you buy (and read) it every day or every month, subscribe. If not, and you have Internet access, see if you can do without.

Found money: $_____

• *Books*: Low priority. Use the library.

Found money: $_____

• *CDs/music/videos/DVDs*: Low priority. You can build your collection at another time.

Found money: $_____

• *Grooming expenses (manicures, haircuts)*: Low priority. Other than getting a haircut when you need it, this is one category that can be slashed to nearly nothing. The $10 you spend on a manicure every week adds up to $520 toward your debt (or savings) by the end of the year. So . . . learn how to do your own nails, straighten your own hair (I did), tweeze your own eyebrows and wax your own legs.

Found money: $_____

• *Pets*: Medium priority. Before you give in to your child's pet craving, understand the expense you're tak–ing on. The care and feeding of a cat or small dog can run to $700 or $800 annually; for large dogs, double that. If you're trying to minimize expenses, not venturing into pet ownership at all (save, perhaps, a goldfish) is a smarter move. If you already have a pet, you can minimize their prescription drug costs by buying medications through your own drug store or on-line rather than through your vet. Local pet stores holding clinics for simple health-care needs like shots will be cheaper than making a vet appointment. Buy food in bulk at warehouse stores or on-line.

Found money: $_____

• *Other*: The same rules apply. Pare back where you can; do without where you have to.

Found money: $_____

Found money from variable expenses:

$_____

Total found money (fixed and variable):
$_____/30 days per month

TOTAL FOUND MONEY/DAY: $_____

So, how did you do? Did you find your $10 a day? Did you find more? If so, that's terrific. You can move on to step 9, page 159, which will tell you how to make sure that money gets where it needs to be. If you didn't free up enough cash, go on to step 8, page 141. There we'll talk about other ways to free up the necessary money: making some hard choices, selling assets, earning more.

Find the Money: Making Hard Choices, Selling Assets, Earning More

⌁

WHAT IF YOU GET through this exercise and you don't free up enough money to make ends meet? Then you have three choices. You can go back through some of the bigger-ticket items in the prior chapter—the ones you thought were nonnegotiable— and try to reduce them further. You can go through your home and your possessions and see if there's anything of value to sell by having a garage sale, listing items on Web sites like eBay or using a consignment shop or broker. You can try to earn more money, either on your current job—or more likely—by taking on a second one. The other alternatives? Credit counseling and bankruptcy. You're not there yet. We'll get to those drastic measures toward the very end of the book. For now, let's see what else you can accomplish on your own.

Making Hard Choices

Sometimes cutting back on what you're spending on lattes and lunches is all you need to do to make ends meet. Sometimes that doesn't make a big enough dent, and you need to look at the line items that are costing you the most money: housing, your car(s), education. Your own detailed listing of your expenses will open your eyes to the areas that are hurting your chances of paying back your debts and becoming wealthy. It's time to take a closer look. Among the things you may want to consider:

Moving. Is your housing sabotaging your ability to make ends meet? I know it's hard to hear, but it is for a lot of people. During the last decade or so, we were so afraid that if we didn't buy *right now* we'd be priced out of the only neighborhood we wanted to live in. We were afraid that if we didn't bid *so much* for that charming three-bedroom cape, we'd lose it. Just as we lost the last four houses we wanted. But it may be that selling your house is a solution you have to consider. I know the conventional wisdom is that your house is the asset you'll retire on (and often retire in), that it's the most valuable asset in your portfolio. But unless you can afford to make the payments, it's also the one that can be your Achilles' heel. It may be *necessary* to trade down—swapping a larger house for something more manageable and less expensive. But you also may need to consider renting for a while. As long as you can keep the cost of moving reasonable (recruit your friends), renting will save you the cost of homeowners insurance. (You'll need renters insurance, but it's much cheaper.) You'll save on yard care and—depending on where you relocate to—you may be able to cut your commuting costs as well. The nice thing about renting now is that, over the last year or so, the cost of renting has fallen by about 10 percent while the cost of owning has gone up by about 20 percent. The gap between the two has gotten wider. This explains why there are so many very nice rentals sitting empty—and so many landlords cutting deals. In other words, if this is the decision you have to make, now is a pretty good time to make it. I'm not saying that you shouldn't own a house. Owning a house and paying it off is a big step toward wealth and financial security. I'm saying that if you can't make ends meet, you perhaps shouldn't own *this* house at *this* time.

Getting rid of a car. There probably is—if you dig down deep and consider it—another less-expensive way for you to get back and forth to work each day. By going without a car for a while, you could save the cost of paying for the car itself, its upkeep, gasoline, auto insurance and parking. And if you can't go without, how about trading in your pricey car for one that runs just fine but is used and less luxurious. I understand that making both of these choices seems like a huge hassle, but every hard choice you make requires some form of sacrifice. If you haven't been able to bring your budget in line so far, the question is not whether you're going to have to make hard choices; it's *which* hard choices are you going to make.

Putting your children in public school. The thought of moving your children from one school to another can be overwhelming. (For some of us, the thought of taking just about anything valuable from our kids elicits the same reaction.) But I just want to tell you—from experience—that it's not so bad. I moved four times when I was growing up, and as a result I went to elementary school in Wisconsin, middle school in Indiana and high school in West Virginia. I griped each time. Between

Wisconsin and Indiana I may have thrown an all-out fit (I've blocked it out), but in reality, it wasn't terrible. In fact, changing schools taught me that I could make friends just about anywhere and gave me the confidence to choose to go away to college in Pennsylvania and then move (on my own) to New York for a job. My point is that your kids won't like the thought of this one bit, but if you sit down with them (if they're old enough to understand it) and explain that this is the only way you have a shot of helping them (financially) attend college, chances are they'll eventually come around. And even if they don't come around before they start at their new school, by the time they've made the basketball team or gotten a part in the school play, they'll be sold.

Clearly, there are many more hard choices that you may want to ponder. But these three examples are here to give you an idea of what you can accomplish if you open your mind to the possibility of doing things differently—like taking the bus or walking to work— even if it's just for a little while.

Selling Assets

When big corporations are looking to lower debt and boost profits, one of their primary strategies is to sell assets. They sell divisions, product lines, inventory, equipment. You can do the same on a smaller scale. What possessions do you have that might be valuable on the open market? Which could you part with if it meant financial security? Your boat? Second car? Second home? Time–share? Art or jewelry? I understand that a lot of these things have strong sentimental and emotional value. Selling them might not be easy. In fact, it might be heartbreaking. But stop to consider how much of your time you're spending worrying about the financial corner you're in now. Perhaps, despite the fact that it's a sacrifice, the trade–off involved in selling some valuables is worth it. If so, you need a strategy to get the most for them.

- *Know what they're worth.* Whatever you're selling, it's important to have an accurate idea of its value before you let it go. If you're talking about a car, that means consulting guidebooks like the Kelley Blue Book or its Web site, KBB.com. If it's a piece of jewelry or another valuable item, you'll want to get it appraised by a certified appraiser. The key to getting an *accurate* appraisal is hiring an appraiser who is not in the business of selling the item. If the appraiser could possibly sell the item, he or she has a financial incentive to undervalue it. That would enable him to make more on the transaction. If it's a household item that's not worth having appraised, you can get an accurate idea of fair market value by seeing what similar items are selling for in classified advertisements or on eBay.

- *Consider where you're likely to get the best price.* It may not be where you think. For example, the best prices on used cars rarely come to you via a dealer trade-in. These days dealers make so little money on new cars, they're having to make it up on used cars (i.e., your trade-in), financing and service. You may do better selling it yourself—but there will be the aggravation of advertising it, showing it and having people come to your house to see it.

- *Decide whether you'll sell it yourself or use a broker.* Just as there are real estate brokers to sell homes, there are individuals who will sell just about anything for a cut. Professional estate sellers and liquidators (in the phone book under "liquidators") will come in, assess what you have to sell and tell you if they can get rid of it for you—though they typically won't take lots worth less than a few thousand dollars. If you're dealing with smaller potatoes, and you don't want to go it alone, you can use individuals—often with eBay's "power seller" designation—who will auction off your merchandise on the Internet. You hand it over; they hand you a check for 50 to 70 percent of what they net. The big question is, do you have the time and inclination to do it yourself? If not, by all means, hand it over, make the money and put it to better use.

- *Whatever you're selling, take the time to make it look good.* If it's a car, clean it thoroughly (consider having it professionally detailed if you can come up with the cash), clean the engine as well and have your local body shop take out any noticeable dents or scratches. If it's an item you're selling on eBay, make sure you post a good-looking photo (or perhaps several) taken from different angles.

- *Be cautious about the transaction.* Don't take a personal check. Accept cash, cashier's checks or money orders only. If a buyer tells you they need a day or two to obtain that cashier's check, make sure you get a deposit in cash. After all, if you've advertised well, this is when you'll have the steadiest stream of buyers.

How to Have a Great Garage Sale

There are entire books written on how to make the most money from a garage sale. But the body of advice seems to boil down to a few commonsensical tips.

- *Start with a plan.* Pick a date at least a few weeks out. Weekends are best—Saturdays first, Fridays second, Sundays third. Steer clear of weekdays, holiday weeks and weekends and anytime close to April 15, when people are worrying about paying their taxes. You might as well start in the early morning. That's when people are going to show up anyway.
- *Go through your house and decide what goes.* A good rule of thumb: If you haven't used it in two years, you can live without it. But don't throw anything away. Even if you think it's junk, someone else collects it.
- *Treat your sale like a business.* Organize the merchandise, putting like with like, so buyers can find what they're looking for. If you're selling clothing, put it on a rack or string up a clothesline and hang it for people to see.
- *Advertise.* Run ads in local papers, on the Internet (there are lots of free yard- and garage-sale sites) and put up flyers. Be specific about what sort of merchandise you have: clothing, antiques, whatever. You'll get the people who really want that stuff.
- *Spend time on your signs.* Much garage-sale traffic just follows

the signs, so make sure you write in large, legible, block print on large, strong oaktag or foamcore. Make your directions clear ("¼ mile on left"). Then take your signs down after the sale is over so your neighbors don't get annoyed.

- *Consider joining forces.* In the world of garage sales, more is better. If you're not sure you have enough to fill your yard, collaborate with a few families. To keep track of who's earned what, put different-colored price tags on each family's items. Then make sure whoever's minding the register knows the code.

- *Be prepared to haggle.* Keep that in mind as you attach price tags to your merchandise. If you're firm on a particular item, write that on the tag as well, as in "$75 firm." If you see that items aren't going at their original prices, drop prices through the day to get rid of as much as you can.

- *Don't forget to . . .* check with your town or village to see if you need a permit (you might). Mark your house clearly—as if you were having a birthday party—with balloons or signs. Don't take checks. Have plenty of change and small bills on hand, as well as old grocery bags and newspaper for wrapping. Post a sign near the register that says "All Sales Final." And on a hot day, sell cold sodas for $1 a can. That should substantially boost your take.

- *Donate anything that's left.* Stuff that remains can be donated to the Salvation Army, Goodwill, Big Brothers or another local organization. You can take a tax deduction for the fair market value on this year's return. If you don't know what something's worth, consult the Goodwill Web site at Goodwill.org, eBay to see what like items are selling for or a book/software program called Cash for Your Used Clothing, available at itsdeductible.com.

Earning More

I know—you work hard already. But sometimes the only way to dig out is by earning extra money. You may be able to do that on your own job. If it's been a year or more since you received a raise, it's time to ask for one. If you don't get it, ask your supervisor what you need to do to increase the size of your paycheck.

If that doesn't work, you may need to get a second job. Eight and a half million Americans have already done so—four out of ten of them, according to the Bureau of Labor Statistics (BLS)—to meet regular household expenses or pay off debt.

There are certainly some primary jobs that are more moonlighting-friendly than others. According, again, to the BLS, the workers who moonlight most often (generally because of flexible working hours) are: firefighters, physicians' assistants, announcers/ disk jockeys/broadcasters, specialty artists and performers (like calligraphers and circus clowns) and therapists and marriage counselors. The general rule, if you're considering moonlighting, is to clear it with your primary employer. Many companies don't have written policies on moonlighting, but whether or not yours does, you don't want to cause tension with the employer that's providing you (and perhaps your family) with health insurance. There may be something your current employer can do to increase your income, whether it's increasing your hours or your responsibilities. But you'll never know unless you ask.

Looking for a second job is much like looking for a first. Read want ads and surf job boards, but be sure to check out temporary services as well. Although job growth heading into 2004 was anything but strong, temporary hiring continued to show gains. Temp services don't just place people from 9 to 5, either—they cut across all occupations, and around the clock. If you're a temp, you don't have to worry that you'll let someone down when your financial situation has improved and you're ready to leave.

Tales of Life and Debt: Kitty

For four years in the late 1990s, Kitty, a 36-year-old office manager, was married to a man who was a financial fiasco. More to the point, he just didn't have a clue about the toll debt could take. Her new hubby came out of law school with $120,000 in student loans and promptly decided he didn't want to be an attorney. Both of them had jobs, but they found it tough to live below their means. Kitty's husband spent more than he earned on toys and other gadgets. He took on a $25,000 car loan. He'd often charge on her credit card without her permission, Kitty recalls.

She could have handled all of that. What she couldn't handle was that when she tried to talk to him about his spending problem, he wasn't willing. "He wouldn't sit down with me to figure out how to get out of this mess," she says. In the end, she decided she couldn't live with someone so financially incompatible with her. So she left, leaving him with the student loan and taking the rest of the debt on her shoulders. She started a new life in Alaska, of all places.

Kitty knew that if she wanted to have a financial future, this time around it would have to be different. So she took the first job she was offered—waiting on tables in the morning and busing tables into the night. It wasn't glamorous, but it was lucrative. She kept spending to a minimum. "I shop sales, pack lunches, don't dine out much, don't buy a lot of clothes," she acknowledges. The process worked. She cleared the credit card debt. Within a year, she was able to pay off her car.

By 2001, she'd had enough of the restaurant life and found an office job. Even though the debt was gone, she continued to live a frugal lifestyle that enabled her to start saving. "I never used to have savings—ever," she says. "We always lived paycheck to paycheck." But she found that having money in the bank gave her a level of comfort, a feeling of stability.

It also enabled her to buy a home. Kitty saved $10,000 for a down payment and bought a $171,000 fixer-upper in the town of Juneau in the summer of 2003. She got an interest rate of 5.25 percent—an affirmation of the fact that her credit score was excellent. Then she went about furnishing the place via her local thrift stores. "I couldn't afford to buy new," she says. "Even a cheap bedroom set in Juneau is about $1,500 because everything has to be brought in on a truck. I probably spent a total of $1,000—on everything. And it's really cute, really nicely furnished."

She didn't stop there. She has $1,000 in savings in the bank in case of emergencies, and lines of credit available to her in case that's insufficient. In 2004, she opened an IRA with a substantial deposit. She's managed to make room to spend money on the things that she really enjoys—like Lancôme cosmetics and expensive cologne.

The best part is that these days she sleeps really well at night. "I didn't sleep for six months during my divorce. I lost 33 pounds, and it was extremely stressful," she says. "But now things are going along fine. I feel good because I have a backup plan for everything."

Tales of Life and Debt: Dan and Sarah

Dan and Sarah were both liberal arts students. He wanted to be a poet; she wanted to run a restaurant. "I guess like spirits do attract," he muses. Both came out of graduate school with a heap of student loan debt and credit card debt. So they moved to Boston, found the cheapest apartment possible and tried to live on their all-too-small entry-level salaries. He was 30 years old, making $23,500 at a public relations firm ("I made more as a bellhop at the University of Virginia," he gripes). She was a few years younger, managing a restaurant, making even less.

"We were kind of spinning our wheels for a few years, financially," he recalls. The money came in. The money went out. Both self–admitted food–and–wine geeks, they ate more of it than many people might have. But they believed life was meant to be enjoyed. Then one day they took stock. Dan, in particular, saw his fortieth birthday closing in. They wanted to buy a house—sooner rather than later. They wanted to have a baby. They decided to change their financial lives. "We knew that if we didn't come up with some sort of plan, we could waste another 5 or 10 years and nothing would happen. We might have had better jobs and better pay, but we still would have had the same financial problems."

So they mustered their courage. "It was hard," says Dan. They made an appointment with a financial planner. He put together an initial plan to guide them on the path to reducing their debts and start saving. The first few steps were very basic. They called their credit card companies and asked for a reduction in their interest rates. Their Discover card lender dropped the rate from 18 percent down to less than 10 percent. "That was the easiest thing to do," says Dan. "It gave us enough quick gratification that we knew that we could actually make a dent in this thing." They made some small adjustments in their spending; Sarah stopped buying clothes for a while. Eating out became a special occasion, not an everyday occurrence.

But the other steps they took—and choices they made—were much harder. They decided to live without a car. Walking to work and traveling longer distances via public transportation saved them thousands of dollars a year. They decided they needed to make more money. Dan took a look at his field—high-tech PR—and he could see that there was a growth curve in the industry and in his company. He believed that if he put in his time, there was an opportunity to prosper. But not for Sarah. So she switched careers, taking a page from her husband's actions and pursued a job doing PR for a software company.

After working extra hard, including weekends, to outperform expectations on the job, Dan and Sarah started to put some serious money away. As they were digging out of debt, both became avid participants in their companies' 401(k) plans. They were able to achieve every one of their goals. Fast-forward to 2004: Dan and Sarah own a house in the Boston suburbs, and they have a beautiful baby girl. "It all came together in a pretty powerful way," he says.

STEP 9

Pay It Down — Intelligently

Who Gets Paid First?

When it comes to paying off your credit cards, there's only one basic rule: Pay the highest interest rates first. I know there are differing opinions on this. Some people say you should pay off the smallest debt to get rid of one card faster. I've heard others say that when you get a great balance-transfer offer, you should start paying on that card so that you make headway while you have access to those low interest rates.

Both are wrong. You pay off your highest-rate debts first because those are the ones that are costing you the most. Let's say you have four credit cards and that you owe a total of $12,000. For simplicity's sake, we'll say you owe an equal amount on each. That gives you:

Card A: $3,000 at 24 percent

Card B: $3,000 at 18 percent

Card C: $3,000 at 12 percent

And you just transferred your balance onto Card D:
$3,000 at 0 percent

The minimum payment on each card is $60 a month. Since you've been setting aside your $10 a day, you have an extra $304 to put toward the card of your choice.

If you take the cards in order of highest interest rate, paying off A first, then B, then C, then D (while paying the $60 minimum on the rest), it will take you 31 months and cost you $13,684. In other words, you'll be out in under three years. And that's truly impressive.

So, as we talked about in step 5, you call all your credit card companies and see if you can talk your way to lower interest rates. You do all the balance transfer-ring you're going to do (for now at least), then lay all your cards out on the table. Note the interest rate you're paying on each one and that'll tell you where to put your muscle in terms of paying it off.

(*Note:* As you pay down this first card, your mini-mum payment will decrease. Your goal—under the

$10-a-day plan—has been to pay what you were pay-ing before [the minimum] plus an extra $10 a day or $304 a month, but if you maintain the minimum pay-ments you started with and *then* add your $304 a month, you'll get out of the debt hole even faster.)

What If You Can't Pay Everyone?

Then there's this problem: What if you're trying to put away your $10 a day, pay off your bills and build some savings, and you hit a bump in the road? It happens. What are you supposed to do if there's a month or two when you simply don't have the money to pay every-one? Follow these rules:

Necessities first. These are the things you absolutely need to live. You need your house, so it's important to pay the mortgage or the rent. You need it to be warm in the winter and lit year round, so it's key to pay the utility company. You need a phone, so Ma Bell gets paid. You need transportation to work, so you make the car payment. If you owe child support, it's a must-pay not only because that's part of being a good par-ent, but because not paying can get you thrown in jail. And finally, because getting in to see the doctor these days—particularly if you have no health insurance—

requires paying the bill then and there, you take care of medical emergencies.

Uncle Sam second. If you have the money to pay your taxes immediately, the IRS will generally work with you to come up with a schedule of payments. By all means, though, file your taxes when they are due. Not filing can result in penalties and interest of up to 25 percent of what you owe.

Most student loans are backed by the government. That means that, like back taxes, the government is al- lowed to come after these loans in ways that other creditors aren't. If you're delinquent in paying your back taxes or student loans, the government can seize your tax refunds and garnish your wages and, in some cases, your Social Security benefits. Fortunately, the government also has a number of solutions for people who can't afford to make their student loan payments, including putting those loans on hold if you're out of work or stretching out (and thereby reducing) the amount owed each month.

Everything else third. All of your other debts— bank–card debt, department store debts, payments for furniture and appliances—are back–burner debts. That doesn't mean you shouldn't pay them. You bor- rowed the money; of course, you should try to pay them. But if you're in a situation where you know that not every creditor is going to get paid, these are the ones you put on hold.

Once you fall behind on payments, what—gulp!—is likely to happen next? Your creditors will start to call. After a month or so, you'll get a letter demanding payment. At this point, you have a decision to make. If you're in a temporary financial slump, one you could see ending in the next couple of months, it's worth calling those creditors and explaining the situation to see if you can put a halt to the collection process and negotiate better terms for paying back what you owe. But part of the deal will likely be agreeing not to charge any more on your card.

If you can see from where you're sitting that your situation is more long-term than temporary and that an interest rate reduction wouldn't do you much good, it's not going to be that valuable for you to negotiate. You might as well just ride it out. Somewhere in the next three to six months—after you've been 90 days late—your creditor is going to turn over your file to a collection agency. Your credit card company may have called once or twice to try to nudge you to pay, but it's when you become a prospect for a collection agency that the calls begin in earnest. You're now dealing with people who are paid on commission any-where from one-third to one-half of any money they can get you to ante up to your credit card company. That's why they're so relentless.

But just because they're the loudest, it doesn't mean that they should be paid first—or even second or third. Even though they call you day and night, they still come after your true needs and government-related obligations. Why? Because other than damaging your credit rating and your credit score (not the best scenario in the world, but also not the worst), there's very little these lenders can do to you. There's no collateral behind the money you owe them. There's nothing they can even try to take from you. They went into business with you—lending you more money than perhaps you could withstand—knowing that. They made a calculated bet on you. They knew they were going to lose a certain amount of money each year on clients who, when push came to shove, couldn't afford to pay. For now, it's their loss.

Once you've found your $10 (or more) each month and decided where it's going, the challenge becomes getting that money out of your hands and into the hands of your creditors, your savings account or your brokerage account before you have the chance to spend it.

You can try to do this yourself, but I wouldn't. If you're late on a single payment—just one—to a credit card company, you can see a relatively sane interest rate soar into the mid-20-percent range. By far the best way to be sure that your money gets where you want it to go is to use some form of automatic transfer.

The good news is that moving money around automatically is now easier and cheaper than it's ever been before. It's tough to find a financial services provider that *doesn't* offer you some way to do this. They're not fools. They've read the writing on the wall and it says that automatic payments aren't only the wave of the future, they're the wave of the present. Americans already make more payments automatically—by credit card and debit card in addition to electronic bill payment—than they write checks. And that number is growing fast.

Consumers have caught on to the fact that automatic transfers are hugely convenient. According to research from Javelin Strategies, it takes an American household about 2 hours to pay by hand the 10 to 12 bills it receives each month. Automating everything (after the setup) can cut that down to about 15 minutes. That's why even people who only begin by paying a couple of bills electronically are soon paying them all that way.

Let's talk about how this would work in practice. You go to work and earn a paycheck. That paycheck gets deposited (direct-deposited, preferably) into your checking account. You know that you want that money to go toward repaying, say, your highest-rate Visa bill. Because you're no longer racking up new charges on that card, you know about what you'll be paying on that card—the minimum, plus the additional $10 a day. Now you can schedule an automatic transfer into that account on a date that's convenient for you (perhaps right after you receive a paycheck) but before the bill is due. And you can schedule minimum payments to pay the rest of your cards, your mortgage, car loan, and any other bill you pay regularly.

You can do this through your bank. Most offer bill payment services, and many, because they're so eager to have customers switch to electronic bill payment (cheaper for the bank than processing checks), offer it for free. If you want in on this party, it's important to understand that you're not locked in to bill payment only through your bank—though for many people that sort of consolidation makes sense. Here's a look at your electronic payment options, and their natural fit:

Direct debiting. By far the easiest solution, direct debiting is when you authorize one of your creditors to reach its electronic fingers into your checking account and pull out a certain amount of money every month. In practice it works best when the payment is fixed, as it is with your mortgage, health club dues, car payment, even utilities—cases in which you balance your bills every month for consistency, then settle up at the end of the year. If you're not ready to go fully on-line but want to take a step in that direction, start here. The downside: If your balance isn't fat enough to cover these withdrawals, you'll get hit with late and over-limit fees. Once you have paid back your creditors and are moving money into a savings or brokerage account instead, this is how you'll schedule deposits into those accounts. You'll authorize your bank or brokerage firm to pull out the money before you have the opportunity to spend it.

"Biller direct" payment. Many credit card companies and other big billers allow you to go to their Web sites and pay your bill. It requires some setup—you generally need a user ID and password—but after that it's very easy. You can see your most recent statement

on-line, as well as other recent transactions, and can choose how much you want to pay, from the minimum to the entire balance. Print a receipt for yourself, and you're done. One of the big benefits is that this is something you can do down to the wire. In many cases, the payment can be posted the day you make it (though sometimes billers charge for this). If you go through a bank, it takes a couple of days. By coupling biller direct with direct debiting, you can sizably reduce the number of checks you write without fully automating. The downside: You have to travel from site to site to pay your bills.

One-stop bill payment. Your other option—and in my opinion your better option—is to pay your bills at a single site. You can do this through your bank, but there are other players in this market as well, like Quicken, CheckFree and AOL. The big benefit of one-stop bill payment (beyond the one-stop convenience) is that it will allow you to see your account balances before you write checks and allow you to do everything from one site. The catch is that there's sometimes a fee of anywhere from about $7 to $11 a month. That's particularly true with the third-party sites. Most large banks, however, waive the fee for either the first six months or for customers who maintain a particular balance. As I write this, Bank of America and Citigroup, two market leaders, have made on-line bill payment free for everyone.

Once you pick a solution, there's setup to contend with. If you're going the one-stop way, that means entering your account information and the name and address of the creditors and other billers you regularly pay. You can choose which day of the month each bill will be paid, which account you want the money to come from (checking or money market) and even—for bills that run the same amount month to month—schedule payment of bills in advance. The one caveat: You still have to keep a careful eye on due dates, or at least build in a buffer. Money doesn't move from your bank to your biller instantaneously. If your biller is set up to accept electronic payments (most companies are), it can take up to three days. If your biller isn't set up to accept electronic payments (many individuals aren't), your electronic bill-payer will send a check through the mail, which can take five days before the money gets into their hands.

Finally, there's one other benefit of going high-tech, no matter how you do it: Just as filing your taxes electronically dramatically reduces the error rate, so does paying bills electronically. The fewer human hands touching your paperwork, the better. Still, it's your responsibility to be sure the proper amount of money has been transferred or withdrawn.

What if you're a technophobe? What if the thought of all these electronic transfers gives you the heebie jeebies? You know you can trust yourself—once you've freed up all that money—to parse it out by check. The old-fashioned solution is fine as long as you stay on your toes. The American Bankers Association just surveyed 1,000 folks on their ATM usage, and 37 percent said they never—*ever*—use the machines. It's a good bet they prefer to pay their bills by hand as well. Just set up a series of reminders for yourself. Mark the dates your bills are due on every calendar in the house. If you use an electronic organizer or calendar program, schedule pop-ups to prompt you to pay as well.

STEP 10

How to Deal When Things Go Wrong

⟳

THERE MAY be times along this road to wealth when things go wrong. It's my wish for everyone who picks up this book that you'll find your $10 a day, put it to work for you and be able to stop worrying (at least about your money; I can't do anything about the time you spend fretting over your kids) forever. But I'm enough of a realist to know that although I can wish it, it's not going to happen for everyone.

Some people will suffer the same sorts of bumps in the road that got them in debt to begin with: health scares, divorces, unemployment, spending that's beyond their control. If you're one of the people who find yourself in deep trouble, I want you to have the information and resources you need to handle it. Here's some advice to get you started on dealing with a shopping problem, creditors that won't stop calling or a pending foreclosure of your home.

Do You Have a Shopping Problem?

Do you hide purchases—or receipts for purchases? Do you buy things in cash so your spouse won't notice? Do you get a craving if you haven't shopped in a while? And a high when you actually buy? Is every trip to the mall followed by feelings of guilt—then yet another round of cravings? Do you buy things to punish your spouse or the other people in your life?

If the answer to one or more of these questions is yes, then you may very well have a shopping addiction. The thing about a shopping problem, unlike a drinking problem or a drug problem, is that it's so easy to mask. Even highly addicted shoppers seem to be smart (they're certainly smart about getting a good deal), well-educated, certainly well-dressed people—and they're participating in an activity that's completely acceptable. It's social. You can do it with your friends.

How do you deal with a shopping problem? As you do with any other addiction—by getting help. There are therapists who specialize in dealing with financial issues. Marriage/couples therapists tend to be particularly strong in this area because money problems are such a big threat to relationships. Some antidepressants have proven to be effective in dealing with shopping disorders. There are also 12-step programs, run by not-for-profits like Debtors Anonymous, as well as by for-profit therapists that can help you deal with the underlying causes of your shopping/debt problem and give you the support you need to get through. You can find a Debtors Anonymous group near you on the Internet at www.debtorsanonymous.org.

When You Need Credit Counseling

What if you've made it through this book and you still can't make ends meet? You've tried to reduce your interest rates, find extra money, sell assets, get a second job...and it's just not working. It's time to consider other solutions. Credit counseling is one of them.

Credit counselors use a formalized approach to debt collection. They work for you by putting clients—for whom they decide it is appropriate—on something called a "debt management program," or DMP. If you apply for, and are accepted into, a DMP, your credit counselors will arrange for you to pay off your debts at lower interest rates. (How much of a break they are able to net you varies by creditor, not by counselor, not by client. Card issuers have a schedule of the breaks they're willing to give to counselors and they don't vary from those schedules.) If you go into a DMP, late fees and other penalties you've assessed will also be waived, which for many clients can be more of a relief than the interest-rate break.

In exchange, you will agree to stop using your cards and you will agree not to apply for additional credit. From this point on, rather than writing checks each month to your creditors, you'll make one payment each month (usually electronically) to your counseling firm. The counselor will, in turn, distribute the money to the creditors you owe. For doing this, your creditors will rebate a portion of the money (known in the industry as a "fair share contribution") to your counseling firm. But DMPs aren't free to you either. You'll pay both a monthly and upfront fee.

How do you know whether you should consider counseling? You should, if you:

- Are using one credit card to pay off another.
- Are taking out cash advances because you don't have cash.
- Have asked for an increase in your credit line and been denied.
- Have lost track of how much debt you have.
- Are using your credit cards to pay for groceries because you don't have the money.
- Are worrying about money constantly.

Unfortunately, credit counseling is a field—like many others—in which you can't trust every person or group that advertises that it can help you. We are just coming out of a period in which large credit counselors have been investigated by the Federal Trade Commission, sued by various attorneys general and called before Congress to testify. You don't need to worry about the minutia as much as you need to understand this: You can't assume every credit counseling group is any good. You have to look at each one individually, check it out and make a decision about whether or not you believe they can help you.

How do you know if a counseling organization is credible? Having not-for-profit status is a good start, but it's not enough. So:

- Look in the Yellow Pages to see that the organiz-ation is recognized by the Better Business Bureau.
- Call the Better Business Bureau to be sure there's no history of consumer complaints.
- Ask the organization if it's a member of the Na-tional Foundation of Credit Counselors (NFCC) or Independent Association of Credit Counselors. Both use only certified credit counselors.

When you've narrowed your list, ask the counselors these questions to make your final decision:

Ask: What do you do?

Bad answer: We "consolidate debts" or put people on "debt management plans."

Good answer: We'll evaluate your financial situation to see what sort of solution is right for you. The coun-selor can't know whether your finances are appropri-ate for a DMP until he or she has been through them. Your situation might be good enough that you can work through it on your own—or so bad that a DMP won't help and you need a bankruptcy attorney.

Ask: How much time will you spend with me in an ini-tial consultation?

Bad answer: Less than half an hour.

Good answer: A half-hour or more. [It's impossible to figure much out in less than a half-hour. An hour is an even better answer.]

Ask: What kind of debt do you help people with?

Bad answer: Just credit card debt.

Good answer: All kinds of debt; we even have a housing counselor on staff who can help you deal with your mortgage. You don't just want a counselor to deal with your credit cards if your car loan, student loan and mortgage are causing you worry as well.

Ask: How much will this cost?

Bad answer: More than $75 upfront. More than $35 a month.

Good answer: Less than $75 upfront. Our monthly payments are on a sliding scale, but you won't pay more than $35 a month.

Dealing with Debt Collectors

Credit card delinquencies are at an all-time high. That's been good news for debt collectors because it means business is booming. It's expensive for corporations to try to chase you down on their own, so after a few (often cursory) in-house efforts to try, they hand your file over to a debt collector who earns a certain percentage of whatever they can get you to pay in commission. Some debt collectors play purely by the rules, but others are cowboys who have little trouble pressuring you, antagonizing you, frightening you, calling you at all hours of the day or night—in fact, doing whatever they can to get you to ante up.

That's why complaints against debt collectors have been steadily rising. The Federal Trade Commission received more than 15,000 in 2001 (the last year for which data is available) and that number has been growing by about 10 to 15 percent a year. Another measure of the steadily rising number of complaints: The number of lawyers in business to handle them. A decade ago, there were two attorneys processing suits against collection agencies. Now, according to the National Consumer Law Center, there are more than 100.

How do you know if a debt collector calling you has gone too far? Generally, you'll know it in your gut, but it helps tremendously if you understand what they are and are not allowed to do to get you to pay. According to the Fair Debt Collection Practices Act (FDCPA) of 1977, collection agencies are *not* allowed to:

- Call you before 8 A.M. or after 8 P.M.
- Use deceptive, unfair or abusive practices when try-ing to collect their debts.
- Threaten litigation if they don't have the right to sue you (creditors have the right to sue, collectors don't).
- Lie to you if they're trying to collect a debt by telling you they're going to throw you in jail or contact your boss.
- Call you on the job if they know (because you're a teacher, for example) that it's not possible for you to take these calls at work.
- Call you on the job if they know your employer has prohibited it.
- Threaten to garnish your wages (they can't do that unless they have a judgment).

Understanding those ground rules, what's the best way to deal with them?

Hang up the phone. You don't have to talk to a debt col-lector. And you don't have to return their calls. Many consumers make the mistake of trying to reason with debt collectors. If you know that what you're being called on is a debt you didn't accrue, call the credit re-porting agencies and get a copy of your credit report, which will help you to get to the root of the problem.

Ask the collector to cease contact. Make it clear to the person on the phone that you would work with them if you could, but right now, you can't do that. Then ask the collector to cease contact because it is causing you distress. That's important, because when you tell the collector they're causing you distress, they are supposed to stop.

Put it in writing. Unfortunately, it's not enough to ask that a collector stop calling; you need proof that you did it. Taping the call is legal in some states—but not every state—so you're better off getting the name and address of the collection agency or creditor calling you, and writing to them. You can use the letter on the following page or write your own. Again, the point is to ask them to stop calling because it causes you distress. Then send your letter certified mail, return receipt requested. Collection agencies have to stop when they get such a letter. Creditors don't, but often if they get the feeling that you are truly upset, they'll start worrying about being sued for harassment, so they'll stop as well.

Get a lawyer. If you're being harassed, there are now a significant number of lawyers in this country who will represent you. Settlements aren't generally for a ton of money—they start at $2,000 or $3,000 and go up from

Letter to Collection Agency to Cease and Desist

Date
Your name
Your address
City, State, Zip

Name of Person at Collection Agency
Collection Agency Name
Address
City, State, ZIP
RE: [*insert account number*]

Dear [*name of agent or agency*]:

I am writing to request that you cease and desist in your efforts to collect on account number [*xxxx*], for [*$ amount of debt*]. I will resolve this matter with the original creditor, and do not want to be contacted further, by phone or mail, by a collection agency.

This is in compliance with the laws of the Fair Debt Collection Practices Act. If you fail to comply with this notice, I will file a formal complaint with the Federal Trade Commission as well as my state's Attorney General's office.

Sincerely,
[*Your signature*]
[*Your typed name*]

there. That's because debt collectors know that unless you can prove you've been damaged by their actions—that you've lost a job, for example, or suffered mental breakdown—the most you'll be awarded in court is $1,000 plus attorneys fees and costs. But you can try. For a list of lawyers, try the National Association of Consumer Advocates Web site, www.naca.net.

Avoiding Foreclosure

Americans are having a tougher time than ever making their mortgage payments, according to a survey released in early 2004 by the Mortgage Bankers Association. Its data showed that a record 1.23 percent of mortgages, some 640,000 loans, were in the foreclosure process. That's not only a significant jump over the 1 percent of loans in foreclosure at this time in 2003; it's the highest rate in 30 years of record keeping. Not surprisingly, the number of homeowners more than 30 days late on their payments—though not yet in foreclosure—also jumped.

What's behind the leap? Unemployment, largely, but also the fact that more credit has been available in recent years—even to people who have had trouble paying their bills. Also, appreciation in the real estate market has been a factor. The prospect of easy gains have lured people into buying bigger homes than they could really afford.

The good news is that chances of *avoiding* foreclosure are also greater than they've ever been. Fannie Mae is now working out solutions to 53 percent of problem loans, a sizable jump over the 35 percent it was working out five years ago. Other lenders are following suit. That's because nobody wins in a foreclosure. The borrower gets a bad credit record and the lender spends time and a lot of money—an average $2,500—going through this process.

What should you do if you're feeling pressed? First, understand what *could* happen. Miss three payments and a "breach letter" will arrive from your lender signaling you're in violation of your contract. You then have a month to respond. Let that month go by and the lender has the right to "foreclose," which means they take ownership of the house.

Letting that three months slip past is the biggest mistake homeowners in trouble make. Instead, here are the steps you should follow:

Call your lender, immediately. Explain why you're having difficulty making payments, how long that difficulty will last and what will have to happen in order

for the problem to resolve itself. Be prepared to provide financial details—including monthly income and
expenses. The goal here is to get lenders on your side
in helping you to solve your problem. So don't wait
for the lender to call you. If you call them, they'll see
that you're not trying to shirk your responsibility.

Refinance. If you have yet to miss a payment, refinancing can lower your payments in a number of
ways. You can lower your interest rate, extend the
term of your loan (thereby stretching out your payments) or convert some of the equity in your home to
a cash cushion you could use to get by.

Ask for partial payments. If you have an FHA loan, your
lender may be willing to allow you to make a partial
payment—paying $700, for example, instead of the
full $1,000 you owe—for a short while without chang-
ing the terms of your mortgage. You generally can't do
that with a conventional Fannie Mae or Freddie Mac
loan. But if you call and say you've just missed a payment, your lender will generally tell you that you can
make up that payment by spreading it over the next
few months.

Look at a loan modification. If you know that you're not
able to continue to pay at the current rate but that you
can pay something, your lender will generally try to

work with you to come up with a payment that you can afford. This is called a loan modification and it works a bit like a refi without going through that process. You'll pay back what you owe, but you may do it over a longer period of time, or at a lower interest rate, or after a short break in your payment schedule to allow you to get back on your feet.

If, after considering all of these alternatives, staying in your house doesn't look possible, try these two fixes; neither will protect your house, but both can protect your credit rating. The first is called a "preforeclosure sale." It will allow you to sell your property (while living there) and move on in an organized fashion. The second is called a "deed in lieu of foreclosure." That's when you give back your house to the lender and the lender disposes of it.

Tales of Life and Debt: Recovering from a Setback

Chris, an entrepreneur based outside Atlanta, sent me this message. I couldn't tell his story better, so I decided to let him tell it himself:

My wife and I are responsible, hard-working, dedicated and giving people. We both paid our way through school. It took me 10 *years to earn my degree. I joined the navy reserves, used loans and at times worked four jobs. We both graduated in 1994 and we still have $23,000 in student loan debt.*

In 1995, I closed a business (a business I did not belong in) with about $160,000 in debt. We never declared bankruptcy and eventually paid back what we owed in 1998. Over the next few years, I focused on my career. It seemed that every two years, I took a better job and we would move.

In 1999, we ended up in Atlanta. We thought we had finally made it. I had a great job as operations director of a large hyperbaric medical center. And my wife got her first position as a kindergarten teacher for a private school. We bought a house, new cars and had our first child. We started investing in our own retirement accounts and saved. We paid off our credit cards monthly. We were finally on track and trying to live within our means.

Toward the end of my first year, my employers were not living up to the contract we had, especially in the area of my bonus. This continued to be a problem, but I was reassured that it would be resolved. In February 2002, my employers tried to add to the contract they weren't honoring and I put my foot down. So they resolved the issues by firing me. To date they owe me about $35,000. I will never see it because it will cost too much to pursue.

Now we were off-track again. I was collecting unemployment. My wife made $20,000. We had no health insurance, a mort-

*gage, bills and a new baby boy. We lost most of our retirement ac-
count during the crash. Still, we took care of the necessities, including new health insurance. As a result we have racked up—to
date—over $20,000 in credit card debt.*

*I kept looking for a new job, but I was discouraged. After a
few months, I told the unemployment counselor that I was going
to start my own business placing and managing hyperbaric
medical services (a business that I do belong in). I wrote my own
business plan, drained our emergency fund, acquired an SBA
loan and acquired a nine-year contract with a medical facility.
The doors opened in January 2003 and we have been growing
slowly and helping lots of people. I was able to pay myself a
small salary after the sixth month.*

*So here we are in January 2004. I have been in business for
one year, in which my company made over $100,000. I plan to
double the business at the first facility and add two more facilities
this year.*

*Right now all the bills are being paid at home and with the
company. But they are far from being paid off. Our goals are to
get rid of our personal credit card debt, increase our savings and
retirement accounts, pay off our student loans and save for college. This past weekend I received great news. My wife told me
she is pregnant with our second child. We are very happy about
this and it now motivates us to do more about our financial
future.*

Let's take a look at what happened in Chris's life. After a rocky start, he was making smooth financial progress—paying down his debt, saving for the future. Then he lost his job. Particularly over the last few years, that's been one of the biggest reasons Americans have gone deeper into debt (health problems and divorce are the other two).

But Chris didn't give up. He regrouped. He thought long and hard about his skills and how he could best use them to make enough money to dig his family out of its hole. Having done it once before, he knew that although it would take time—and very likely be difficult—he knew it was possible. So he started, one step at a time. Now, nearly two years into the process, he's well on his way. He has even more faith in his ability to take care of his family of four, now and in the years to come. And I'm right there with him. This is a guy who knows that slow and steady progress wins the race every single time.

STEP 11

Staying Ahead of the Game

Y OU'VE MADE IT—through the book and into the
program. I'd like to be able to tell you that you're
finished, that you're done. You're not. Steering clear of
debt and building wealth is a lifelong endeavor. And
right now the key is keeping your head above water.
There are a few very important habits you can adopt to
stay out of debt. These habits are here to help you make
the most (i.e., actually enjoy) your newfound financial
freedom without sinking back into some destructive
behavior patterns. They're here to help you protect
what you've built—because as you now understand,
this sort of freedom is a luxury that not too many people enjoy—as well as to help you on your journey.

Staying Out of Debt

For the record, one more time: I don't think there's anything wrong or bad or evil about credit cards. I think they're a flexible spending tool that, when used wisely, can make paying for the things you need to buy in this life much easier and much more convenient. You know you're using them at least fairly wisely if you can adhere to these two golden rules for credit card customers:

- Always pay more than the minimum.
- Always pay on time. Remember: One late payment can send your interest rate soaring.

If, however, you occasionally have trouble with those two rules, or you find yourself sliding back toward that minimum payment habit, it's time to find another means of paying for your purchases. Two suggestions include:

Debit cards. The use of debit cards has been growing steadily. More consumers today opt to pay with debit cards than with credit cards. Smart folks. Debit cards, which draw money out of your checking account whenever you make a purchase, don't allow you to overspend in the same way that credit cards do. In the scheme of things this is a huge advantage. Huge. Bigger than huge, in fact. Enormous.

But there are a few key differences between debit and credit that you should be aware of. First, if you use debit, you lose the float. If you use a credit card, you generally have 20 to 25 days to pay the bill. During that time, the money is yours to use, not the merchant's. Use debit, and the money is spent. Second, you lose some of the safety. If a credit card is stolen, you cancel it and, while you're liable for the first $50 of purchases you didn't make, most card issuers are waiving that nowadays. If your debit card is stolen, a thief could clean out your checking account before you even realize what's happening. Yes, your bank will give you back the money—many will issue an immediate credit so you have money to spend while the paperwork is being processed—but it's generally a bigger hassle than canceling a credit card. Finally, third—a distant third—you lose the miles. Now, I want to note: Miles are only a good deal for people who pay off their credit cards every month.

Stored-value cards. For some people debit cards don't offer enough protection from their desire to spend. Why? Because they allow you to spend everything that's in your checking account at the time—money you may need for other uses. Some even allow you to go overboard. The overdraft protection on your checking account kicks in to cover whatever amount you "borrow" and you're faced with fees and interest. If you've found debit cards don't work for you, try a stored-value card instead. These look like credit cards and work like a combination of credit/ATM card, but the limits of your spending are finite. You load the card with whatever amount of money you choose— some employers are starting to offer stored-value cards in lieu of all or part of your paycheck (a boon for people who don't have bank accounts)—and spend it down (or use it to get cash from an ATM). When the money is gone, it's gone. Using the cards isn't free. Fees run anywhere from about $3 a month to about $6, but that might be a price worth paying if it's the only way to keep yourself in line.

Starting to Save: The Eleventh Dollar

The other key to staying ahead of the game is saving. You need a savings stash to keep you from sliding back into debt. Think about it: You're moving along, putting aside your $10 a day, paying down your credit cards, making terrific progress. Then your dog gets a nasty double ear infection. Between trips to the vet and strangely pricey medications, this ends up costing you close to $200. Where is that money going to come from?

Unless you have a stash of savings, you're going to put it on your credit card. And although you now know enough to put it on your lowest rate credit card, that purchase is going to set you back. It's going to impede your progress. And it's going to make you feel rotten. That's why you need savings.

Phase two of this program—after you've used your $10 a day to pay off your credit cards—is to take that $10 a day and stash it in a safe place, the highest paying money-market account you can find (go to bankrate.com to find the best rates today) until you've got a substantial emergency cushion. You want one equivalent to three to six months' living expenses. That's your protection. If you get laid off, if the dog gets ill, if your transmission dies, you'll be able to live and pay your bills without sliding back into credit card debt.

But what about during phase one—while you're still focusing your energy on paying down that credit card debt? *You still need to save something.* So the question becomes: Where do you get that money? Here are a few suggestions.

Windfalls. There are times when money falls into your lap. You get a bonus, a small inheritance, a tax refund. Put that money away. Don't spend it. Consider it a down payment on whatever emergencies come later.

Raises. If and when you get a raise—even if it's just a few dollars per paycheck more than you were making previously—don't spend that money either. Arrange a direct transfer of the precise amount of additional cash that's showing up in your paycheck from checking and into savings. Think about it logically—you were living without that cash before. If you start spending it immediately, it will be no time (I promise) before you can remember how you ever lived on less. But if you pretend it's not there, you can use this raise to help your savings grow.

The eleventh dollar. Many of you, when you went through the process of finding money, ended up with a number bigger than $10 on the bottom line. I know $10 is what we were reaching for. But if you got to $11 or $12 or $15 or $20, I don't want you to put the excess toward your debt until you've accumulated your cash cushion. Again, arrange for a direct transfer of whatever additional money you found into savings. If you hit $10 on the nose, I want you to go back and find *one more dollar a day*. That's $365 a year to bail you out of a jam. What if you drew blood the last time around and feel you simply can't go back to the well? Then put this savings cushion together the old-fashioned way: with cash. Every day, take a dollar out of your wallet and put it into an emergency fund. Better yet, take your dollar and your change. I promise you, you won't miss it. And when Fido starts scratching his ears uncontrollably, you'll be very glad it's there.

Protect Yourself from Disaster with Health and Disability Insurance

There are two other things that could sabotage your ability to stay ahead of the game: a health scare and a disability. As you work toward financial independence, it's important to insure yourself against both of these possibilities. They may never become realities—I hope in your case that they don't—but the point is, you can't know. And unless you're protected, either one of these scenarios can ruin you. Not just in the short term but for years to come. Here's how to buy both in the most cost efficient way.

Health insurance. The leading cause of personal bankruptcy is not wasteful spending or reckless investing but unpaid medical bills. That's surprising, but only until you consider that at any moment some 40 million Americans are without health insurance and another 40 million have experienced a gap in coverage sometime over the past two years. If you are laid off and work for a company with more than 20 employees, you can, by law, maintain your health coverage through your former employer's plan under a law called COBRA (the Consolidated Omnibus Budget Reconciliation Act). But at an average $600 a month, it's also expensive. The good news is, if you're in reasonably good health it's getting easier to find affordable health insurance on your own—particularly on-line.

You'll want to start on the Web, where—according to eHealthInsurance.com, the on-line market leader, a healthy family of four (thirtysomething parents and school-age kids) can get a major-medical plan—with a $1,000 annual family deductible and copayments of $30 per doctor's visit and $10 for generic drugs—for about $400 a month. The price falls to $200 a month with a $5,000 deductible. A healthy 30-year-old single male can pay about $160 a month, or $50 with the higher deductible. You'll have to go through medical underwriting, answering health questions and opening up your medical records. Depending on what's there, an insurer may want to charge a higher rate or exclude existing conditions. In such cases, COBRAing might be a better deal.

If you think that within the next 6 to 12 months you'll be back in the workforce, think about a short–term policy. Short–term policies are cheaper because they exclude coverage for existing medical conditions and reimburse a smaller percentage of your costs. Besides eHealthInsurance.com, go to Fortis Insurance (fortishealth.com), the leader in this part of the market.

Before you buy anything you find on the Web, however, you'll want to get a second opinion. So take your Web quotes to an insurance agent who can assess your needs, explain complex policy riders and sometimes get you a better deal. (Some insurers aren't in on–line databases.) You can search for agents in your area through the National Association of Health Underwriters at nahu.org. You want one who specializes in selling coverage to individuals.

Check out association coverage. Many institutional and professional groups, including alumni associations, offer well–priced coverage to members. But don't assume that your group has chosen a good company. Before signing up with any insurer, see whether its customers lodge a lot of complaints: go to "Consumer

Information Source" at www.naic.org, the National Association of Insurance Commissioners' site. Check quality ratings at www.ncqa.org, the National Committee for Quality Assurance site. And before using an insurer based out of state, ask your state's insurance department whether you'll be protected if the company tries to raise your premium but not those of other policyholders.

Finally, consider a health savings account. Hidden in the new Medicare bill is a gift for people under age 65 who want to cut their health insurance bills. It's called the health savings account (HSA), and many experts believe these accounts will revolutionize health care. HSAs started rolling out onto the market in 2003. What do you need to know to understand if one might be right for you?

How they work. HSAs are a little like IRAs. You buy a qualified health insurance policy with a minimum deductible of $1,000 for singles, $2,000 for families. That enables you to open a health savings account, into which you can deposit pretax dollars up to the level of your deductible each year (capped in 2004 at $2,600 for individuals and $5,150 for families). You don't have to deposit a lump sum all at once. Generally, you'll be able to make monthly deposits by automatic debit.

Once the money is in the account, it's yours to spend—tax free—on health care. If you don't use it, your money can remain in the account and grow tax deferred. (We'll get to your investment choices momentarily.) That gives HSAs a leg up on flexible spending accounts (FSAs), where you lose any funds you don't use within the year. If you withdraw money before you reach age 65 for things other than IRS-approved health-care expenditures, it will be taxed as income and you'll pay a 10 percent penalty. At age 65, the penalty vanishes. At all times, though, the money in the account belongs to you. If you change jobs, you can take it with you.

What kind of health insurance you'll get. So far, most HSAs are set up with preferred provider organizations (PPOs) that offer you discounted rates on a network of physicians and hospitals until you reach your deductible and cover 80 percent to 100 percent of in-network bills after that. These are basic policies, with some limitations on coverage.

How you open one. Some employers are planning to add HSAs to their menu of insurance options at open-enrollment time. Right now most HSA policies are being purchased by people who are self-employed or who don't have insurance at work. A good place to start looking for a policy is, again, eHealthInsurance.com, which in mid–2004 already offered 140 different policies in 26 states.

How you pick a good one. Shop around, paying particular attention to how easy it is to access your money. Plans that come with checkbooks or debit cards are easier to administer than those that make you file paperwork to get reimbursed. The other deciding factor: your investment options. Some plans offer a fixed return on any money you deposit in the account. Others allow you to invest the money in a menu of mutual funds. Whether you want to put your health–care dollars at risk depends on whether you have other reserves.

Bottom line. If you already have a high–deductible individual policy, adding an HSA is a no–brainer for the tax savings alone. Otherwise, it may be a good bet if you're basically in good health. You should consider one if you've been paying more for health insurance premiums than you've been using in care. Take a typical family of four in San Diego, who would pay $828 a month for a traditional PPO with a $500 deductible. Premiums for an HSA policy with a $4,800 deductible would run $226 a month—a savings of $602 a month or $7,224 a year. If the family puts $4,800 into an HSA, that still leaves them with savings of $2,424 a year. And assuming they pay 34 percent in combined federal and state taxes, they'd save $1,632 more on taxes. Even if they spend every dollar of the $4,800 they put into the account, they come out way ahead.

Disability insurance. Your chances of becoming disabled than dying before you reach age 65 are six times as great. Disability insurance is particularly important for single people who have no one else's income to fall back on but their own. If you're single and you get injured and are unable to work, there will be no money coming in to pay your bills unless you've planned ahead and gotten this coverage. (To find the money, if you're single and paying for life insurance, cancel it. Singles who don't have dependents relying on them for financial support *do not need* life insurance.)

What's the most cost effective way to purchase this coverage? Through your employer. Most company policies will only get you a portion of the coverage you need, however. Optimally, a disability policy should replace 60 to 70 percent of your current income. Payment should kick in if you're unable to work in your "own occupation" rather than just any occupation. This is really important. Say you're a surgeon and you injure your hand. You would be unable to perform your own high-paying job. But unless you have "own occupation" coverage, the insurer may be able to make a case that you could work in a job that didn't require such dexterity (maybe on the register line of a fast-food joint) and certainly wouldn't pay as much. Other benefits—such as inflation protection—are less important.

Disability insurance isn't inexpensive. But you can bring the cost down by extending the waiting period between the time you become injured and the time coverage kick in. Extending the waiting period from the standard 30 days until 90 days can mean a significant reduction in price. You can shop for disability insurance on the Internet, but should also talk to an agent who specializes in these policies. Get at least three quotes from top-rated insurers (Moody's, Standard & Poor's or A.M. Best) before you buy.

Protect the You Everybody Else Sees: Monitor Your Credit Report

By December 2004 every consumer is entitled to receive one credit report free each year. Details on how those reports will be distributed were still being worked out as this book went to press, though it looked as if they would be disseminated through the three major credit bureaus.

Until that time, you're entitled to a free report if you've been turned down for credit, employment or insurance based on information in your credit report. You have 30 days to file your request. Make sure to include a copy of your denied application. You can also get a free report if you're unemployed, receive welfare assistance or believe you've been a victim of identity theft. You can also get one free report a year if you live in Colorado, Georgia, Maryland, Massachusetts, New Jersey or Vermont. Otherwise, you'll be charged up to $9 depending upon the state in which you live.

You may not like the idea of paying some firm one cent for information that was—in actuality—yours to begin with. But letting the relatively small charge stand in your way of getting your hands on a truly crucial document would be a very big mistake.

Checking your credit report once a year is the *very best* way to be sure you haven't been a victim of identity theft. If you have, you'll often see on your report credit cards and loans that have been taken out in your name but don't belong to you. It's also key to check your credit three to six months before you apply for a mortgage or a car loan. This gives you a chance to clear up any misinformation before the lender pulls your credit report and score for himself. If you've been lax about paying your bills, the three- to six-month window also gives you an opportunity to show the creditor that you've turned the situation around.

Here are the addresses, phone numbers and Web sites of the three major credit bureaus, as well as Fair Isaac, where you can pull all three. Again, if you're only going to pull one, pull the one that has the likelihood of giving you the fullest file: Equifax in the South and Southeast, TransUnion in the North and Northeast and Experian in the West.

TransUnion
P.O. Box 390
Springfield, PA 10964–0390
800–916–8800
www.tuc.com

Equifax
P.O. Box 740241
Atlanta, GA 30374–0241
800–685–1111
www.equifax.com

Experian
P.O. Box 949
Allen, TX 75013
www.experian.com

What to Look for on Your Credit Report

A recent study from U.S. PIRG showed that 70 percent of credit reports—nearly three-quarters!—have at least one error. The first time I pulled my report I found a doozy on mine. The bureau had included information on my report from another Jean Sherman (my maiden name) who lived in Brooklyn (as I did at the time). Only this Jean Sherman had a lien on her house. It was curious to me that an error like this could be made—as an editorial assistant at the time, earning about $13,000 a year, I could hardly afford a house. The silver lining is that most of these errors are not the sort that put someone else's lien on your report. They tend to be more administrative.

That's why, as you go through your report, pay particular attention to:

• Your identifying details including name, Social Security number and date of birth

- Addresses, current and former
- Employers, current and former
- Accounts, are the correct ones listed as active and closed
- Records of late payments
- Bankruptcies (which must be removed from your record after 10 years), suits, judgments, tax liens, and arrest records (which must be removed after 7 years)

How Do You Dispute Information on Your Credit Report?

Back when I found the problem on my credit report, I had no choice but to correct the information sloooowwwly. By snail mail. Today you can dispute information on your credit report either by mail or on-line. If you do it by mail, the credit bureau will send you a form to fill out or you can simply write a letter or use the one on the next page.

What If the Bureau Won't Remove the Information?

If after investigating your claim, the credit bureau agrees with you that the information is incorrect, it must remove the information and then send you a copy of the accurate report. If the credit bureau doesn't agree that the information should be removed, you can write a letter—or, again, use the one I've provided—explaining your version of events and ask that the credit bureau attach it any time your credit report is pulled. Until the matter is settled, a creditor can't give out information that would hurt your credit standing with potential creditors or other credit bureaus.

Letter to Dispute Information on Your Credit Report

Date
Your Name
Your Address
Your Social Security Number

Name of Credit Reporting Agency
Address
Attn: Complaint Department

Dear Sir or Madam:

I am writing to dispute inaccurate information in my credit record. The creditor is [*name*] and the account number is [*xxx*]

This item, dated [*day/month/year*], is [*inaccurate or incomplete*] because [*I did not purchase the product* or *the amount is inaccurate* or *there is a mathematical error* or *the product or service was not delivered as agreed*]. I am requesting that the item be [*deleted or corrected*] from my credit report.

A copy of my credit report with the disputed item highlighted and circled is attached. I am also enclosing [*any supporting documentation such as payment records*]. I am also requesting that this letter be kept on file as a permanent part of my credit record.

Please investigate this matter with the creditor in question and [*delete or correct*] the disputed items as soon as possible. If you have any questions, I can be reached at [*daytime and night phone numbers*]. Thank you for your prompt attention.

Sincerely,

[*Your signature*]
[*Your typed name*]

Enclosures [*list attached items*]

Letter to Be Attached to Your Credit Report

Date

Name of Lender
Address of Lender

Dear Sir or Madam:

I am applying for a mortgage/loan with your company, and I am writing to explain the [*missed loan payment/bankruptcy/default/other credit problem*] on my credit report. The information in question is circled on the attached copy of my credit report.

[*Explain what happened and why you were in financial difficulty: because of unemployment, illness, or other reasons.*] Fortunately, this problem has now been corrected [*because you found a job, etc.*] On my credit report, you will notice that I have now amassed a [*year or however long*] track record of on-time payments, and have no other outstanding credit issues. In addition, I do not anticipate a recurrence of this problem in the future.

Please attach this letter to my loan application file. I hope you will take this explanation into consideration when reviewing my mortgage/loan application.

If you need further explanation or information, please do

not hesitate to contact me at the address below or by phone [*daytime and evening phone numbers*].

Sincerely,

[*Your signature*]
[*Your typed name*]
[*Your address*]
[*City, State, Zip*]

Afterword: Congratulations

HERE YOU ARE at the end of *Pay It Down!* I hope that along the way you were able to free up some cash and put it where it would do you the most good. I hope that you leave this book—and this exercise— feeling more optimistic about your financial future.

I look forward to hearing how you're doing. Your stories guide me as I work to explore the financial successes and problems of people all across the country (and come up with creative solutions to the latter). So please let me know by writing me at Jean@Jean Chatzky.com. I'll do my best to answer as many of your letters as I possibly can.

And remember...managing your money isn't rocket science. It's making good choices, developing good habits and sticking to them. I know you can do it. I have faith in you.

Jean Chatzky
February 2004

Acknowledgments

A BIG THANK YOU to all the people who helped pull this book (and the coordinating projects at *Money* magazine and at NBC's *Today* show) together. I couldn't have done it without you: Richard Pine, Adrian Zackheim, Richard Heller, Heidi Krupp, Stephanie Land, Bob Safian, Denise Martin, Sheryl Tucker, Eric Schurenberg, Tom Touchet, Betsy Alexander, Patricia Luchsinger, Nancy Kay, Richard Liebner, Carrie Cook, Cybele Weisser, Will Weiser, Amy Wolfcale, Amy Mahfouz, Allison Sweet, Megan Casey, Kimberly Gaynor, Lysa Price, Andrew Federici, Sue Basalla, Jenny Baird and Carolyn Bigda. I'm grateful to the experts who shared their knowledge: Scott Mitic, Keith Gumbinger, Scott Bilker, Robert D. Manning, Steve Tripoli, Elizabeth Warren, Craig Watts, Ryan Sjoblad and John Ulzheimer. Thanks, too, to the people who are always on my side: Diane and Ken Adler, Jan and Dave Fisher, Elisa and Jamie Brickell, Kathy and Arlen Goldberg,

Rob Densen, Wally Konrad, Nancy Pine, Lisa Greene, Susan Kleinman Wechsler, Debi Epstein, Marc Fried, Marcia Meyers and, of course, my family, the Shermans, the Chatzkys, the Lindes, the Meyers and the Nelsons.

Index